TERRY JAMES

NEARING MIDNIGHT

As It Was in the Days of Lot

DEFENDER

CRANE, MO

Nearing Midnight: As It Was in the Days of Lot
By Terry James

Defender Publishing
Crane, MO 65633

© 2024 Defender Publishing
All Rights Reserved. Published 2024

ISBN: 978-1-948014-75-5
Printed in the United States of America.

A CIP catalog record of this book is available from the Library of Congress.

Cover design by Jeffrey Mardel
Interior design by Pamela McGrew

Unless noted, all Scripture references are from the King James Version.

In loving memory of family-close friends Bob and Vicki Rogers,
who, through their daughter, Angie, continue to contribute
so much to my work and especially to my personal life.

Acknowledgments

I am blessed beyond measure to have such a family around me while I advance into the years and continue to present books and commentaries for the Lord's purposes.

My love to Margaret, Terry, Jr., Nathan, Kerry, Dana, Jeanie, and all of the grandchildren with whom the Lord has blessed me.

To my editor, Angie Peters, my deep love and thanks for her wonderful work, and most of all, for her daughter-closeness through all of our books together. She and Kurt continue to mean so much to my life.

To Todd Strandberg, my love and admiration for his faithfulness in trusting and obeying the Lord as God directs his paths in founding and continuing to put forth truth through Raptureready.com.

To my Christian brothers and sisters Tom Horn, Donna Lee, and all the wonderful friends at Defender Publishing for their superb book publishing expertise and production, my most profound gratitude. We have grown in the Lord together over these years of efforts for His great purposes.

To Daymond Duck, my close friend of many years and among the very best writers and presenters on Bible prophecy in the world today, my brotherly love and deep thanks for the foreword to this book.

To friends who have been readers of these volumes over these many years, you are always in my thoughts. I derive spiritual strength from your silent, though keenly sensed, presence.

To my Savior and Lord, without whom nothing of value could be found in me: my love, absolute thankfulness, and total devotion.

CONTENTS

Section I
PERILOUS TIMES

Section II
MIDNIGHT MADNESS

Section III
SODOM AND GOMORRAH GODLESSNESS

Section IV
DELIVERANCE

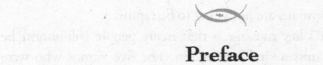

Preface

By Todd Strandberg

THE TERM "NEARING MIDNIGHT" is actually an odd reference to the pre-Tribulation Rapture. There is no set date for when the Lord will come for the Church. He could come at 8 p.m., 10 p.m., or 3 a.m. We are told by Jesus the Rapture will be a complete surprise:

> Watch therefore, for ye know neither the day nor the hour wherein the Son of man cometh. (Matthew 25:13)

The real point of reference for "nearing midnight" is the Tribulation hour. For more than two decades, our Rapture Ready website has featured on its home page the image of a digital clock that is set to a couple of minutes away from midnight. Someone might criticize the process of "nearing midnight" as being extremely slow. I have no frustration with the timing, because the signs of the time tell us the Rapture is very near.

Another common prophetic term, "midnight cry," is closely related to "nearing midnight." Jesus said "the kingdom of heaven" will "be likened unto ten virgins, which took their lamps, and went forth to meet the bridegroom" (Matthew 25:1). All the virgins fell asleep, and at midnight, there was a cry that the bridegroom was there. Five of the virgins had extra oil for their lamps and the other five were running out of oil.

The five foolish women went to buy more oil and missed meeting the bridegroom. Most people focus on this as being a reference to the Rapture. However, Jesus' main point was warning people to be ready. Some argue that "lukewarm" Christians are not going to be raptured.

I think the Lord's key message is that many people will almost be ready, yet they will miss a vital connection. The five virgins who were foolish wanted to meet the bridegroom, but lacked an essential ingredient that would qualify them to join the marriage feast. I've met several people in my life who have had a great interest in Bible prophecy at one time, but who slowly burned out.

I've been writing about biblical prophecy and related issues for more than thirty-five years. I have to admit I do sometimes get bored with some subjects I'm very familiar with. My love for prophecy never fades, though, because I know it is the reality that takes priority over everything. I can tell we are getting very near to midnight, and the warning cry is about to be sounded.

Before the horrors of this seven-year period begin, Jesus will come down from Heaven to rescue true believers. This a reality Christians should never take lightly. If there were no Rapture, we would be at the mercy of a system that will seek to destroy all who follow Christ.

I never understood why some people who promote a post-Rapture view of the Tribulation would have a positive attitude about going through those seven terrible years. The Bible says humankind will be as rare as fine gold by its end. Nearly all the key Rapture Scriptures use positive phrasing to describe this event, stating it is the "blessed hope," "victory" over death, and something we should view as a "comfort" to one another.

An anti-Rapturist once wrote to me, "We're not going anywhere. We're going to stay here and fight the Antichrist." This is delusional talk. God promises some level of protection to the Jews, and two-thirds of them will be wiped out. When the Lord addresses Tribulation saints, He tells them to prepare to face death:

There before me was a great multitude that no one could count, from every nation, tribe, people and language, standing before the throne and in front of the Lamb. They were wearing white robes and were holding palm branches in their hands. (Revelation 7:9, NIV)

When John asks who these people are, he is told:

These are they who have come out of the great tribulation; they have washed their robes and made them white in the blood of the Lamb. (Revelation 7:14, NIV)

Jesus said His return should be our primary focus. I've found that you can often tell a person's spiritual state by how open he or she is to the Rapture. Some who claim to be believers argue that the Rapture will not happen for another million years. Many see earth as being a better place than Heaven.

Other folks plan to make their end-time arrangements when they get to the end of their life. This strategy fails on two key points Again, we don't know the time of the Rapture, and most people don't know when they are going to die. One of Satan's greatest tools he uses to deceive people is convincing them they have plenty of time to make decisions about eternity.

I've studied Bible prophecy since the late 1970s. When I was in my youth, I was satisfied with the possibility of the Rapture occurring at any time. Lately, I've become very anxious about the Rapture. This world has become such a terrible place that I want to leave now.

I can only watch about ten minutes of news each night. Many times, the content of the broadcast is so predictable that I turn off the TV after just hearing the previews. (I've made life better for myself by not watching any prime-time programming. I get my entertainment "fix" by watching YouTube videos from a purer time: British documentaries from the 1980s, science news shows that cover current events, and game shows from the 1950s.) Our nation glorifies freaks and weirdos; teachers talk to students about sex; many of our key cities allow criminals to roam free; and mass-murder events take place almost weekly. We're cursed with the dumbest group of leaders who have ever held office. Washington has spent so much money we now have levels of debt that will eventually destroy America.

Usually when a nation falls into gross immorality, the result is the downfall of that nation. Because the Rapture is a "timeless" event, I believe God is holding back calamity until after He removes the Church.

Anyone who still has any love for this world needs to reassess his or her faith. If a doorway to the Kingdom of Heaven opened up, we should enter immediately, without looking back, as did Lot's wife.

Foreword

By Daymond Duck

PEOPLE WHO KNOW I WRITE about Bible prophecy often ask me to recommend writers, books, and websites to them.

Terry James, his books, and Rapture Ready are almost always on my list.

I got acquainted with Terry in the mid to late 1990s when he invited me to attend a prophecy conference with him that would be held by the Pre-Trib Research Study Group in Texas. I met some of the premier Bible prophecy teachers in the world at that conference and others during the following years: Tim LaHaye, Hal Lindsey, John F. Walvoord, J. Dwight Pentecost, David R. Reagan, Grant R. Jeffrey, David Hocking, Randall Price, Zola Levitt, Chuck Missler, and Noah Hutchings, to name just a few. Terry was on a first-name basis with all these great men, and they all knew and respected him. They knew his theology was sound, and many contributed chapters to books that he wrote.

There are very few, if any, Bible prophecy topics that Terry has not been writing about for twenty-five to thirty years. He has studied them all. He has labored over them all. He believes in the authority of Scripture. He challenges false teachings. He encourages people to be faithful. He helps people understand difficult topics in the Bible.

Books like those Terry writes and edits are extremely important. Further, his "Nearing Midnight" commentaries on Raptureready.com are up-to-date and spot on. Most pastors are letting their flocks down in the area of biblical prophecy, so writers like Terry who are experienced and careful to study, teach, and write what the Bible says are badly needed.

Terry's writing will help you. I encourage you to read his books and "Nearing Midnight" commentaries.

As far as this book (*Nearing Midnight: As It Was in the Days of Lot*) is concerned, I am leaving that subject in Terry's capable hands and will focus on information I hope will encourage you to study Bible prophecy.

Seven Basics of Bible Prophecy

1. God knows the future. Paul said, "Known unto God are all his works from the beginning of the world" (Acts 15:18). God knows what will happen before it happens.

2. God reveals the future before it happens. He said, "I am God, and there is none like me, declaring the end from the beginning, and from ancient times the things that are not yet done" (Isaiah 46:9–10). God reveals what He plans to do before He does it.

3. The Bible is full of prophecy; it includes eighteen books of prophecy, including five books called the "Major Prophets," twelve books called the "Minor Prophets," and the book of Revelation. God also put whole chapters of prophecy in the Bible (Matthew 24–25). Depending upon whom we talk to, some say as much as 25–40 percent of the Bible centers on prophecy.

4. Bible prophecy is reliable. God said, "The prophet, which shall presume to speak a word in my name, which I have not commanded him to speak, or that shall speak in the name of other gods, even that prophet shall die" (Deuteronomy 18:20). God's prophets had to be right 100 percent of the time. Putting them to death sounds harsh. But if they were attributing things to God that didn't come from Him, they were speaking for Satan.

5. We have proof of the accuracy of Bible prophecy. The Old Testament records more than three hundred prophecies about the First Coming of Jesus. Some prophecies are repeated two or three times. After the repetitions are removed, the Old Testament still records more than one hundred distinctive prophecies about the First Coming, and all were literally fulfilled.

Peter Stoner, former Professor Emeritus of Science at Westmont College in Santa Barbara, California, calculated the probability of one person fulfilling just 48 prophecies to be 1 with 127 zeros behind it. That is a whopping number. One trillion has just 12 zeros.

With the odds being so great for one person to fulfill just 48 prophecies, one must wonder what the odds would be for one to fulfill all 108 prophecies. Fulfilled prophecy is indisputable proof that:

- Jesus is the Messiah.
- God knows the end from the beginning.
- God is in control.
- The Bible is the Word of God.

6. The Holy Spirit revealed important information to the Apostle Peter about Bible prophecy. He said, "We have also a more sure word of prophecy; whereunto ye do well that ye take heed, as unto a light that shineth in a dark place, until the day dawn, and the day star arise in your hearts: Knowing this first, that no prophecy of the scripture is of any private interpretation. For the prophecy came not in old time by the will of man: but holy men of God spake as they were moved by the Holy Ghost" (2 Peter 1:19–21).

Do not overlook these points:

- Bible prophecy is accurate.
- We are wise to pay attention to Bible prophecy.

- Bible prophecy is like a light; it helps us understand other teachings of the Bible.
- Bible prophecy was given by the Holy Ghost (it is accurate, it's wise to study it, and it's helpful because it was given by God).

7. Bible prophecy is about Jesus. John the Revelator said, "The testimony of Jesus is the spirit of prophecy" (Revelation 19:10b). Every individual, especially Christians, should want to know more about Jesus.

Ten Reasons to Study Bible Prophecy

1. It teaches us accountability. Paul said, "It is appointed unto men once to die, but after this the judgment" (Hebrews 9:27). It also teaches us to prepare for what comes after death. Are you prepared? You must be born again (John 3:7).

2. It changes lives. John said, "Beloved, now are we the sons of God, and it doth not yet appear what we shall be: but we know that, when he shall appear, we shall be like him; for we shall see him as he is. And every man that hath this hope in him purifieth himself, even as he is pure" (1 John 3:2–3) Those who believe Jesus will return soon will give up their sins, stop playing Church, get serious about their relationship with Jesus, and get their affairs in order. Christians, and especially pastors and evangelists would be wise to use a message that God said will do these things.

3. Those who love the Second Coming will be rewarded. Paul said, "Henceforth there is laid up for me a crown of righteousness, which the Lord, the righteous judge, shall give me at that day: and not to me only, but unto all them also that love his appearing" (2 Timothy 4:8). This is the only doctrine mentioned in the Bible that will be rewarded with a crown.

4. Jesus said the lost will be removed from the earth at the end of the age. In the parable of the wheat and tares, we read: "As therefore the tares are gathered and burned in the fire; so shall it be in the end of this age [NKJV]. The Son of man shall send forth his angels, and they shall gather out of his kingdom all things that offend, and them which do iniquity; And shall cast them into a furnace of fire: there shall be wailing and gnashing of teeth" (Matthew 13:40–42)

5. In the parable of the dragnet, Jesus said, "So shall it be at the end of the age [NKJV]: the angels shall come forth, and sever the wicked from among the just, And shall cast them into the furnace of fire: there shall be wailing and gnashing of teeth" (Matthew 13:47–50). Christians should tell the lost what Jesus said. It is very important.

6. It is a topic Jesus' disciples were interested in. Matthew said, "As he sat upon the mount of Olives, the disciples came unto him privately, saying, Tell us, when shall these things be? and what shall be the sign of thy coming, and of the end of the age [NKJV]?" (Matthew 24:3). There's nothing wrong with being interested in Bible prophecy. The disciples asked Jesus questions about it.

7. Jesus wants us to be patient about His return. He said, "For many shall come in my name, saying, I am Christ; and shall deceive many. And ye shall hear of wars and rumours of wars: see that ye be not troubled: for all these things must come to pass, but the end is not yet" (Matthew 24:5–6). He was saying many things must happen before the end of the age arrives.

8. Jesus said He doesn't want to judge the world, but He will eventually do it; the end will come: "This gospel of the kingdom shall be preached in all the world for a witness unto all nations; and then shall the end come" (Matthew 24:14). Love and mercy are why He has waited.

9. The end of the age will come. In the meantime, we should be active. Jesus said in the Great Commission: "Go ye therefore,

and teach all nations, baptizing them in the name of the Father, and of the Son, and of the Holy Ghost: Teaching them to observe all things whatsoever I have commanded you: and, lo, I am with you alway, even unto the end of the age. Amen" (Matthew 28:19–20, NKJV).

10. God is pleased with those who understand the signs and tell His people what they need to do. The Lord praised the sons of Issachar because they "had understanding of the times to know what Israel ought to do" (1 Chronicles 12:32). He revealed Bible prophecy for the good of all mankind.

The Lord mentioned the Second Coming in twenty-three of the twenty-seven New Testament books. He mentioned it in one of every thirty verses in the New Testament. Those who don't believe in the Second Coming don't believe many verses in the Bible, including what Jesus said. Jesus said, "The end of the age will come."

Ten Reasons to Look Forward to the End of the Age

1. Jesus will reign and be worshiped.
2. There will be peace, justice, and righteousness on earth.
3. Satan will be bound and chained.
4. Creation will be restored.
5. Multitudes will get saved.
6. The Jews will be saved.
7. God's covenants with Israel will be fulfilled.
8. Christians will reign with Jesus.
9. Christians will see loved ones.
10. Christians won't get sick or die.

We should look forward to these things and pray for them to happen.

The First and Second Coming in the Garden of Eden

When Satan tempted Adam and Eve in the Garden of Eden, God put a curse on Satan and said He would send a seed of the woman. The seed would bruise Satan's head and Satan would bruise the seed's heel (Genesis 3:15). This is a prophecy of the First Coming of Jesus and the virgin birth. Why? Because there is no such thing as the "seed" of a woman. Men have seed, but women have eggs (Genesis 3:15). The seed of a woman would be a miracle birth.

God also put a curse on Eve: "I will greatly multiply thy sorrow [birth pains] and thy conception; in sorrow thou shalt bring forth children" (Genesis 3:16). This is a prophecy of the Second Coming. The Greek word translated "sorrows" means "travail," "labor pains," "birth pains," etc. Birth pains increase in frequency and intensity as the arrival of a child nears.

Jesus said false christs, wars and rumors of wars, famine, pestilence, and earthquakes are "the beginning of sorrows" (beginning of the birth pains, or the Tribulation period; see Matthew 24:8). Paul said, "For when they say, Peace and safety; then sudden destruction cometh upon them, as travail upon a woman with child" (Like birth pains; see 1 Thessalonians 5:3). This is why many Bible prophecy teachers believe natural disasters will increase in frequency and intensity as the Second Coming nears.

The First Story in the Bible and the Last Two Verses of the Bible

As mentioned above, the Creation account in Genesis mentions the First and Second Coming. In addition, the last two verses of the Bible read, "Surely I come quickly. Amen. Even so, come, Lord Jesus. The grace of our Lord Jesus Christ be with you all. Amen" (Revelation 22:20–21).

Bible prophecy is recorded from cover to cover in the Bible, but many Christians hear very little about it. Many don't realize Jesus is coming back to reign over this world and make it a better place.

Christmas Story: About the First and Second Coming of Jesus

God sent the angel Gabriel to deliver a message to a virgin named Mary. When Mary saw the angel, she was afraid (Luke 1:26–28). Then we read:

> And the angel said unto her, Fear not, Mary: for thou hast found favour with God. And, behold, thou shalt conceive in thy womb, and bring forth a son, and shalt call his name Jesus. He shall be great, and shall be called the Son of the Highest: and the Lord God shall give unto him the throne of his father David: And he shall reign over the house of Jacob for ever; and of his kingdom there shall be no end. (Luke 1:30–33)

Notice that the angel revealed seven prophecies in these verses. The first four prophecies are about Jesus' First Coming:

- Mary would conceive and bear a son.
- Mary's son would be named Jesus.
- Jesus would be great.
- Jesus would be called the Son of the Highest.

The last three prophecies are about His Second Coming:

- The Lord God will give Jesus the throne of David.
- Jesus will reign over the house of Jacob (Israel) forever.
- Jesus will have a Kingdom that will never end.

The first four prophecies were literally fulfilled, so we should expect the last three prophecies to be literally fulfilled as well. God will give Jesus the throne of David (the throne of David was on earth in Jerusalem). Jesus will reign (be King) over Israel. Jesus' Kingdom will last forever.

Lest we forget, Jesus taught us to pray, "Thy kingdom come. Thy will be done in earth, as it is in heaven" (Matthew 6:9–13). Also, Jesus will come back as King of kings and Lord of lords (Revelation 19:16). He will come back to establish a Kingdom on earth in Jerusalem.

My Favorite Pre-Trib Passage

Terry believes in the Pre-Trib Rapture, so I want to give you my favorite passage of Scripture—1 Thessalonians 4:13–5:9—with my commentary. Throughout this section, I've capitalized some of the pronouns to highlight the contrast between believers and unbelievers; the saved and the lost.

But I would not have YOU to be ignorant, BRETHREN, concerning them which are asleep, that YE sorrow not, even as others which have no hope. (1 Thessalonians 4:13)

God doesn't want YOU, the brethren (believers; brothers and sisters in Christ), to be ignorant about what happens to those that have died (those whose bodies are in the cemetery; the word "cemetery" means "sleeping place").

For if WE (the believers) believe that Jesus died and rose again, even so them also which sleep in Jesus will God bring with him. (1 Thessalonians 4:14)

If WE believe in the death and resurrection of Jesus, even though OUR bodies are in the sleeping place (the cemetery), Jesus will still bring OUR soul and spirit with Him.

For this we say unto YOU [believers] by the word of the Lord,
that WE [believers] which are alive and remain unto the coming
of the Lord shall not prevent them which are asleep (1 Thessalonians 4:15).

In other words, Paul said, "We are telling YOU [the believers] what
the Lord [Jesus] wants YOU [the believers] to know about these things.
We [the believers] who are still alive on earth when Jesus comes with
the souls and spirits of those whose bodies are in the cemetery [sleeping
place] will not prevent Jesus from raising deceased believers from the
dead."

For the Lord himself shall descend from heaven with a shout, with
the voice of the archangel, and with the trump of God: and the
dead in Christ shall rise first. (1 Thessalonians 4:16)

Jesus will personally come out of Heaven and raise the deceased
believers from the dead before He does anything about the believers who
are still alive and on earth at that time (see John. 11:43; Revelation 4:1).

Then WE which are alive and remain shall be caught up together
with them in the clouds, to meet the Lord in the air: and so shall
we ever be with the Lord. (1 Thessalonians 4:17)

After Jesus has raised the deceased believers from the dead, all believers
(those who died but have been raised from the dead, and those who have
not yet died) will be caught up (raptured) at the same time to meet Jesus
in the air and be with Him forever. (Jesus doesn't touch down on earth.
Believers will fly away to meet Him in the air).

Wherefore comfort one another with these words. (1 Thessalonians 4:18)

Believers should discuss these comforting words with each other.

But of the times and the seasons, BRETHREN, YE have no need that I write unto YOU. (1 Thessalonians 5:1)

Concerning when the Rapture is near, BRETHREN (believers), Paul does not need to tell YOU (brothers and sisters in Christ) anything about that.

For YOURSELVES know perfectly that the day of the Lord so cometh as a thief in the night. (1 Thessalonians 5:2 esv)

YOU are well aware the Rapture will catch some people by surprise.

For when THEY [the unbelievers] shall say, Peace and safety; then sudden destruction cometh upon THEM [the unbelievers], as travail upon a woman with child; and THEY [the unbelievers] shall not escape. (1 Thessalonians 5:3)

When the unbelievers declare "peace and safety on earth, sudden destruction will come upon the unbelievers, and the unbelievers will not escape (they will be left behind to go through the Tribulation Period).

But YE, BRETHREN, are not in darkness, that that day should overtake YOU as a thief. (1 Thessalonians 5:4)

But YOU, the believers, are not in darkness, so that day will not catch YOU by surprise (you have the Word, and you can see the day approaching).

YE [believers] are all the children of light, and the children of the day: WE [believers] are not of the night, nor of darkness. (1 Thessalonians 5:5; see Matthew 5:14; John 8:12; Colossians 1:12–13)

YOU (believers) have been enlightened by the Scriptures, called out of darkness, and won't be surprised like those who don't believe (1 Peter 2:9).

Therefore let US not sleep, as do others; but let US watch and be sober. (1 Thessalonians 5:6)

Because WE (the believers) are the children of light, WE should stay awake spiritually, watch what is happening in light of the Scriptures, and use good judgment.

For THEY [the unbelievers] that sleep sleep in the night; and THEY [the unbelievers] that be drunken are drunken in the night. (1 Thessalonians 5:7)

Unbelievers are like people who sleep and get drunk at night. They are not aware of what is happening in light of the Scriptures.

But let US, who are of the day, be sober, putting on the breast-plate of faith and love; and for an helmet, the hope of salvation. (1 Thessalonians 5:8)

Let US, the children of light, use good judgment, have faith, love God and others, and cling to our hope that Jesus will come out of Heaven to raise deceased believers, change living believers, give all believers a new body, and take us to Heaven.

For God hath not appointed US [the believers] to wrath [the Trib-ulation period is a day of wrath; see Zephaniah 1:15; Revelation 6:16], but to obtain salvation by our Lord Jesus Christ. (1 Thes-salonians 5:9)

God hasn't appointed believers to go through the day of wrath. He has appointed believers to be saved by our Lord Jesus Christ.

Readers need to understand that Paul is drawing a contrast between WE and THEY, between US and THEM. Christians are a WE, not a THEY. WE are not appointed to wrath, but THEY are.

Premillennialism

When we study Bible prophecy, we sometimes come across big words like *amillennialism* (no millennium), *premillennialism* (Second Coming before the Millennium), and *postmillennialism* (Second Coming after the Millennium). Which is right? The statue in King Nebuchadnezzar's dream reveals that the right answer is premillennialism. It is a timeline that reveals when the Second Coming will take place and when the Kingdom of God will be established on earth.

King Nebuchadnezzar had a dream. He couldn't sleep. He called in his advisors. He told them he had a dream that troubled him. They asked him to tell them the dream so they could interpret it. He couldn't remember the dream, and they couldn't interpret it. Nebuchadnezzar ordered the death of all his wise men, including Daniel.

Daniel asked for time to come up with the dream and its interpretation. He recruited Shadrach, Meshach, and Abednego to join him in a prayer meeting. That night, God revealed the dream and its meaning to Daniel. The next day, Daniel was taken to the king.

Daniel answered in the presence of the king...there is a God in heaven that revealeth secrets, and maketh known to the king Nebuchadnezzar what shall be in the latter days. Thy dream, and the visions of thy head upon thy bed, are these; As for thee, O king, thy thoughts came into thy mind upon thy bed, what should come to pass hereafter: and he that revealeth secrets maketh known to thee what shall come to pass. (Daniel 2:27–30)

Do not miss these three important points:

1. There is a God in Heaven who reveals secrets.
2. God has revealed what shall be in the latter days.
3. God has revealed what shall come to pass.

Daniel told Nebuchadnezzar he dreamed about a great statue. It had a:

- Head of gold (Babylon)
- Chest and arms of silver (the Medes and Persians)
- Belly and thighs of brass (Greeks)
- Legs of iron (the Roman Empire)
- Legs of iron that broke into pieces (the Roman Empire would break up into nations)
- Feet of iron plus clay (the Revived Roman Empire plus other nations)

Daniel said a stone (a rock) struck the great statue on the toes of its feet (Daniel 2:32–42). Then, "the stone [the rock] became a great mountain and filled the whole earth." That rock is Jesus. When history gets to the tip of the toes on the statue, Jesus will come back and establish a Kingdom that will fill the whole earth.

This is the point: The rock (Jesus) will come before His Kingdom is established on earth. That is premillennialism.

Bible Prophecy and the Reality of Angels

Angels are mentioned in the Bible hundreds of times. We know they were created by God (Psalm 104:4); they are spiritual beings that can appear in human form (Genesis 18:1–8); they have names; and they appear and disappear. But is there any evidence of this?

Daniel was praying when the angel Gabriel touched him and said:

Know therefore and understand, that from the going forth of the commandment to restore and to build Jerusalem unto the Messiah the Prince shall be seven weeks, and threescore and two weeks [173,880 days]: The street shall be built again, and the wall, even in troublous times. And after threescore and two weeks shall Messiah be cut off, but not for himself. (Daniel 9:25–26)

Before it happened, the angel Gabriel told Daniel:

- There would be a commandment to restore and rebuild Jerusalem (the commandment is found in Nehemiah 2:1–8).
- Jerusalem would be rebuilt.
- Jesus would appear 173,880 days after the commandment to restore and rebuild Jerusalem.
- Jesus would be crucified.
- Jerusalem and the Temple would be destroyed, and more.

All these things literally happened hundreds of years later in the exact order Gabriel indicated. This is evidence that there really is an angel called Gabriel who revealed these things to Daniel.

Bible Prophecy and the Reality of Heaven

Is there any evidence that Heaven exists? John the Revelator issued several prophecies that would have been impossible when the book of Revelation was being written (such as the Antichrist being able to track all buying and selling, the whole world being able to see the bodies of the two witnesses lying in the street, etc.). But John didn't say he read about these things in the Old Testament; he said he saw them in Heaven.

The fact that these circumstances and events couldn't happen on earth in John's lifetime but are happening now is evidence that John really did see what he reported. The fact that these things are happening now is evidence that Heaven exists.

Prophecies of One Thing

Terry has written a lot about the current situation on earth, so I want to pass on something he may not have covered.

The Bible identifies:

- One nation that will come back into being in one day: Israel (May 14, 1948).

- One nation that will be divided: Israel (the two-state solution is about dividing Israel).

- One nation that cannot be defeated: Israel (several nations have tried to defeat Israel and failed).

- One nation that will be hated by all nations: Israel (there are more resolutions against Israel in the United Nations than against any other nation on earth).

- One nation that will have trees again: Israel (Jews have set out billions).

- One nation vultures will return to: Israel (vultures are migrating from Europe to Africa over Israel).

- One nation the animals will return to: Israel (the wildlife has returned).

- One nation that will have an increase in rain: Israel (more rain is needed, but the rain amounts have increased).

- One nation that will abide many days without a king and a sacrifice: Israel (they don't have a king and are not allowed to sacrifice animals).

- One nation that will return in unbelief: Israel (the Jews have been blinded).

- One nation that will have a pure language: Israel (every Jew is required to learn Hebrew).

- One nation where the plowman will overtake the reaper: Israel (the farmers are double- and triple-cropping).

- One nation that will dominate the descendants of Esau: Israel (the Jews are dominating the Palestinians).

- One nation that will have silver and gold, cattle and goods in the latter days and latter years: Israel (the Jews are exporting oil, natural gas, and cattle).
- One city that will be a "cup of trembling and a burdensome stone" for the whole world: Jerusalem (Israel and the Muslims are constantly fighting over Jerusalem).
- One thing Israel's enemies will claim after Israel returns to the land: the Holy sites.
- One thing that will increase: iniquity (sin—terrorism, violence, pornography, etc.—are increasing all over the world).
- One thing that will decrease: the love of many (the Church is becoming more worldly).
- One thing the gates of Hell cannot prevail against: the Church (and true believers still exist).
- One thing that will spread all over the world: the Gospel (this refers to the two witnesses, the 144,000, and an angel during the Tribulation period, but satellites, television, and the Internet are factors).
- One thing the wicked won't understand at the end of the age: current events (because they ignore what the Bible says; see Daniel 12:10).
- One river that will dry up: the Euphrates (Turkey and Iraq have built seven dams on it).
- One building that will be rebuilt: the Temple (the architectural plans and a materials list are complete).
- One gate that won't be opened until Jesus returns: The Eastern Gate (it is closed and sealed shut).
- One group of nations that will come back into being: The old Roman Empire (that's the European Union).
- One treaty that will be signed: a covenant with the Antichrist (world leaders keep pushing for peace in the Middle East).
- One person who cannot be revealed while the Church is here on earth: The Antichrist (he hasn't yet been revealed).

- One nonhuman thing that will speak: a statue of the Antichrist (scientists are building robots that can speak).
- One religious practice that will resume at the end of the age: animal sacrifices (Jewish priests have been trained to offer animal sacrifices).
- One thing that will speed up at the end of the age: travel (we now have planes and vehicles).
- One thing the world cannot have until Jesus returns: peace (war is a constant problem).
- One thing the world cannot understand: the things of God (because they are spiritually discerned; see 1 Corinthians 2:14).
- One being that won't be bound until the Second Coming of Jesus: Satan (he is alive and well on planet earth today).
- One book that will be sealed up until the time of the end: the book of Daniel (it is a little fuzzy, but current events are making it easier to understand).
- One thing the whole world will see during the Tribulation period: the bodies of the two witnesses lying in the street of Jerusalem (TV and the Internet have made viewing of that possible).

When Jesus announced that one of His disciples would betray Him, He said, "Now I tell you before it come, that, when it is come to pass, ye may believe that I am he" (John 13:19).

When Jesus told His disciples He was going away, He said, "And now I have told you before it come to pass, that, when it is come to pass, ye might believe" (John 14:29).

God revealed the future and is bringing it to pass so we will believe. When we see all the signs, we are to know it is near.

Israel's Blindness

Several people have asked me why God blinded the Jews. In earlier comments, under the section titled "Bible Prophecy and the Reality of

Angels," I pointed out that the angel Gabriel told Daniel the exact day Jesus would appear: 173,880 days after the commandment to restore and rebuild Jerusalem.

Exactly 173,880 days later, two of Jesus' disciples borrowed a donkey and Jesus began what is referred to as His triumphal entry into Jerusalem. A large crowd gathered and shouted, "Blessed be the King that cometh in the name of the Lord: Peace in heaven, and glory in the highest" (Luke 19:38).

The psalmist had predicted the people would shout these words when their Messiah and King rode into Jerusalem (Psalm 118:26). But the Pharisees said, "Master, rebuke thy disciples" (Luke 19:39).

Then a strange thing happened. Luke said, "And when he was come near, he beheld the city, and wept over it." He looked at Jerusalem and said, "If thou hadst known, even thou, at least in this thy day, the things which belong unto thy peace! But now they are hid from thine eyes" (Luke 19:41–42).

Notice the phrase, "in this thy day." This was the 173,880th day—the exact day the angel had said the Messiah would appear. Jesus was saying, "If you only knew the Scriptures, and if you had only believed your confession that I am your Messiah and king, your sins would be forgiven and you would have peace, but you don't know what day this is, and you don't know what it takes to have peace." Then He added, "Now, these things are hid from thine eyes. You will now be blind to these things."

That's something to cry about: religious people who don't know the Scriptures. Religious people who have gone to church all their lives and still don't know the Scriptures. Religious people who don't know the Messiah. Religious people who've been baptized and joined the church before they got saved. World leaders who don't know how to have world peace.

I was present when a friend was talking about the judgment. He held up his Bible and said, "These are the things that are going to be on the test. Don't you think you ought to look at them?"

Jesus said, "For the days shall come upon thee, that thine enemies shall cast a trench about thee, and compass thee round, and keep thee in on every side." He was prophesying that the Romans would surround Jerusalem, attack on every side, trap the Jews inside the city, and:

[Your enemies] shall lay thee even with the ground, and thy children within thee; And they shall not leave in thee one stone upon another; Because thou knewest not the time of thy visitation.

To Sum This Up

If God didn't want us to study biblical prophecy, all He had to do was leave it out of the Bible.

- But God put it in the Bible.
- God told us to study it.
- God said we would be wise to study it.
- God promised to reward us if we study it.

The issue should be settled.

Scripture gives clear warnings about false teachers and false prophets. It is easy to be led astray by those who teach error. Knowing what the Bible says helps us recognize false teachers and false prophets. In Nearing Midnight, Terry draws on what he considers to be his best work and what he believes people want or need to know. His book will strengthen your knowledge and faith. I recommend it to you.

Introduction

THIS BOOK REFLECTS, I prayerfully hope, this present generation as fitting the Bible's description of the people of planet earth at the end of the age—the generation the Lord Jesus Christ foretold while He, in human flesh, walked the small portion of the Middle East now called the Holy Land. If this is that generation, these days so much like the days of Lot in Sodom (Genesis 19) are on the cusp of coming to an abrupt conclusion. A new era will be initiated, leading to the worst time in history, in the words of the One who came to save humanity from sin that separates us from God.

By every metric, the world's inhabitants have reached the midnight hour of human history. But the prophetic horizon is golden beyond all imagination, so don't stop here. Read on!

Listening for the Midnight Cry

The section of our website, www.raptureready.com, in which we put our weekly commentaries is titled "Nearing Midnight." Our purpose is to chronicle issues and events of the current times in order to forewarn that the call of Christ to His Bride, the Church (all those who are born again; see John 3:3) is near.

We can say this with certainty because of the many signals given by those issues and events. These look to be the prophetic signs of the coming Tribulation period—human history's last seven years leading to the return of Christ to earth at the time of Armageddon. Jesus said:

> And when you see all these things begin to come to pass, then look up and lift up your head for your redemption draweth nigh. (Luke 21:28)

Paul the apostle wrote about this moment of redemption:

> For the Lord himself shall descend from heaven with a shout, with the voice of the archangel, and with the trump of God: and the dead in Christ shall rise first: Then we which are alive and remain shall be caught up together with them in the clouds, to meet the Lord in the air: and so shall we ever be with the Lord. (1 Thessalonians 4:16–17)

John, "the beloved disciple," wrote from his exile on the isle of Patmos about his vision of that moment of redemption:

> After this I looked, and, behold, a door was opened in heaven: and the first voice which I heard was as it were of a trumpet talking with me; which said, Come up hither, and I will shew thee things which must be hereafter. (Revelation 4:1)

This shout from Christ, Himself, is likened to the moment when the midnight hour of human history has been reached. The black, boiling clouds of the Tribulation will have shrouded the whole planet in a veil of God's wrath because of humankind's rebellion. We see that moment as represented in the parable of the ten virgins:

> And at midnight there was a cry made, Behold, the bridegroom cometh; go ye out to meet him. (Matthew 25:6)

Nearing Midnight

Despite all the seminary-degreed protests to the contrary, this is the same moment Jesus prophesied in the Olivet Discourse, in what I believe is the most profound declaration about the time He will next catastrophically intervene into human history. I refer to the Lord telling of the coming judgment at the time of the Rapture, as given in the following. Note that Jesus prefaces His prophecy by saying:

> But of that day and hour knoweth no man, no, not the angels of heaven, but my Father only. (Matthew 24:36)

The Rapture is an unknown time; it is imminent—can happen at any moment. The Second Advent can be counted down, because a precise number of days are given to the time Christ returns at Armageddon. The Lord then gives a description of what the world will be like at that unknown hour—an hour unknown by anyone but His Father.

> But as the days of Noe were, so shall also the coming of the Son of man be. For as in the days that were before the flood they were eating and drinking, marrying and giving in marriage, until the day that Noe entered into the ark, And knew not until the flood came, and took them all away; so shall also the coming of the Son of man be. Then shall two be in the field; the one shall be taken, and the other left. Two women shall be grinding at the mill; the one shall be taken, and the other left. Watch therefore: for ye know not what hour your Lord doth come. (Matthew 24:37–42)

Most of my theologically degreed friends—and I love them as my brothers in Christ—say Jesus was addressing the Jews, not the Church, in this passage. This, therefore, has to be speaking the time of His Second Advent at the end of the seven years of Tribulation. However, I believe, as did my good friend, biblical apologist, and author Dave Hunt, that the Lord would not speak confusion into prophecy. At the time of the Second Advent at Armageddon, as many as three-fourths of the world's population will have been killed through the terrible judgments given for that era. People will not be doing what people in societies and cultures do during normal times. And, the time of Tribulation will be by far the worst in human history, according to the Lord's own words (Matthew 24:21).

Hunt spoke about these matters many years ago at a forum I attended. He started his presentation by talking about the title of the topic he was assigned.

> [My] topic is "Is the Rapture in the Olivet Discourse?" Well, I'd like to talk on the topic "The Pre-Trib Rapture in the Olivet Discourse." I couldn't quite handle that question. I couldn't justify why there ought to be any question at all. Why the Pre-Trib Rapture, or the Rapture, or the Church, or anything else was in the Olivet Discourse.[1]

Dave, one of the most thorough and brilliant students of the Bible of my acquaintance, talked then about how the seminary doctoral hierarchy declares that the Olivet Discourse does not address the Church or the Rapture in any way whatsoever. He went on to say the Olivet Discourse, as he understood it, came about in response to specific questions the disciples asked Jesus. They wanted to know when the destruction of the Temple and city would take place, and what the signs of His coming and of the end of the age would be. Dave said Jesus responded with the many signals He gave. Jesus didn't say He was referring to His Second Coming at the time of Armageddon. Dave asked: "Why is it necessary to adamantly say it couldn't be the Rapture Jesus was talking about in answer to their questions?"

A common reason given for the Rapture not being referred to in the Olivet Discourse, Dave said, was that the disciples there with Jesus couldn't understand about the Rapture, because they didn't even understand the concept of the Church at that point.

Dave reminded us that, at another time, Jesus told the disciples He would go away, but would come again and receive them unto Himself, and take them to Heaven, where He will have prepared dwelling places ("mansions") for them (John 14:1–3). The disciples didn't understand this, either, but it was about the Church, and Jesus told them about it. Dave said this coming for the disciples (the Church) couldn't be the Second Advent, because He will return at the time of Armageddon with the saints—including the disciples to whom He was speaking. The disciples didn't understand that, but it is true, Dave said.

But, Jesus was nonetheless speaking about the Rapture. The common sense of the things Jesus was saying fit perfectly—as His teachings always did.

Dave concluded:

> I don't believe His response had to be limited to what they under-stood. But I think He could tell them things that they didn't understand, and not necessarily in a way they would under-stand…. I can't think of any reason—rule of logic or exegesis—that would say the Rapture can't be in the Olivet Discourse.[2]

Jesus expanded on His "days of Noah" analogy to the time He would return at the Rapture:

> Likewise also as it was in the days of Lot; they did eat, they drank, they bought, they sold, they planted, they builded; But the same day that Lot went out of Sodom it rained fire and brimstone from heaven, and destroyed them all. Even thus shall it be in the day when the Son of man is revealed. (Luke 17:29–30)

Be alert! Keep your head up and senses attuned to what the head-lines are saying to your spiritual ears. The midnight cry might be the next words you hear.

Devil's Dementia Goes Viral

Do you ever read, watch, or hear news reports and say to yourself: "The world has gone crazy!" or something to that effect? Certainly, this seems to be a world gone mad. The observation is worthy of in-depth investigation.

Looking in any direction across the landscape of human interaction produces undeniable evidence. This is a planet inhabited by people whose sanity is under assault by an unseen force. It is the same sin sickness that infected the first recorded rebel, Lucifer the fallen one, who is so delusional he thinks he can still defeat the God of Heaven. Thus, I give the malady the designation "devil's dementia." Indeed, it has gone viral upon the earth.

The supernaturally inflicted dementia has brought much of our population to the point that their thinking has become reprobate. The word "reprobate" is defined as "morally depraved; unprincipled; bad." Reprobate thinking is rejected by God and places one beyond hope of salvation (apart from redemption found only in Jesus Christ). It is the kind of thinking with which Satan, the devil, now incessantly assaults God's creation. Humankind is thus fatally infected, with the minds of so many people only focusing on evil continually, just as prophesied.

Jesus said it would be like it was in the days of Noah at the time of His Second Coming (Luke 17:26–27). When we check those days, we find the following:

> And God saw that the wickedness of man was great in the earth, and that every imagination of the thoughts of his heart was only evil continually. (Genesis 6:5)

Let's consider the spreading dementia that afflicts our nation and the world at this late hour in history. Analyzing the arenas of human endeavor and the pervasive upside-down thinking will quite possibly further give us a sense of where this generation stands on God's prophetic timeline.

Religious Dementia

Religion, rather than acting as a comforting abode for the spirit as it is purported to do, more often inflames passions and ignites wars than soothes the savage beast within people's hearts. The most volatile religion of our time has at its very center the demand that genocide be perpetrated upon God's chosen people. *Jihad* is the term for "holy war" that inspires much of Islam. It is sheer insanity to demand that parents strap bombs to their sons and daughters to blow up others in the name of bringing into being peace on earth!

Christianity today more and more spotlights the madness of the hour. Many who say they are Christians have turned from the very reason for Christianity's name—Jesus Christ and His death, burial, and Resurrection as a sacrifice so men, women, and children can be redeemed from sin. False teachers and preachers divert the minds and hearts of people to fables. It is an inward turning toward self-centeredness and away from reaching out to the lost of the world as Christ commissioned His followers to do.

In the name of Christ, Catholicism and evangelical Christianity harbor a seemingly endless number of priests and pastors who abuse their congregants and prey on the innocent children who are supposed to be under their care. This is reprobate thinking and an assault on God—perversion of the worst sort.

The devil's dementia is working within the Church today through the wolves in sheep's clothing, as condemned by Scripture:

Now as Jannes and Jambres withstood Moses, so do these also resist the truth: men of corrupt minds, reprobate concerning the faith. (2 Timothy 3:8).

They profess that they know God; but in works they deny him, being abominable, and disobedient, and unto every good work reprobate. (Titus 1:16).

Socioeconomic Dementia

All we have to do to understand what's going on in bringing down the United States is to consider the American government, the present presidential administration, and the reprobate mind forewarning of Romans 1:28. The strange, almost inexplicable decisions on every level of domestic and foreign policy demonstrate beyond any doubt the dementia that affects US leadership.

These leaders demand that Americans learn to live within their means, yet the politicians run up tabs of trillions of dollars in the drive to convert the nation to European-style socialism at best and a Marxist state at worst. The big tax-and-spenders continue to strap future generations with debt that can never be repaid. Only God's staying hand has prevented the complete implosion of the US and world economies to this point.

All we see happening in society and culture is madness, but it's madness that can be understood as defiantly following the reprobate thinking that opposes the God of Heaven. With a considerable majority of the US citizenry opposing the massive spending spree, the majority party ignores the people's wishes. Instead, they tie to their insane fiscal scheme taxpayer-funded abortions and other anti-God legislation, which enables atrocities such as public schools outlawing Bibles in classrooms while distributing condoms and birth-control pills to students.

The madness spreads and metastasizes.

Although examining this malignancy that's spreading isn't pleasant, it must be done in order to discern the time so near the midnight that will mark the Tribulation hour (also referred to as "Daniel's seventieth week"). I pray discernment will fill each believer who makes the effort to read this book and understand that those who don't know Jesus Christ for salvation will be left on this judgment-bound planet after the Rapture takes place.

We must get this message to these lost souls before it is too late:

That if thou shalt confess with thy mouth the Lord Jesus, and shalt believe in thine heart that God hath raised him from the dead, thou shalt be saved. For with the heart man believeth unto righteousness; and with the mouth confession is made unto salvation. (Romans 10:9–10)

Section I

Perilous Times

1

Lovers of Self and the
Spirit of Antichrist

THIS WILL LIKELY LAND ME IN TROUBLE. The commentary might be pointing the bony finger of condemnation in a direction many will possibly insist it has no right to be poked.

However, we are at the very end of the Age of Grace (Church Age). Every signal for the soon return of the Lord Jesus Christ is becoming more visible by the hour. When we see these things begin to happen, we're told to look up and lift up our heads, because our redemption is drawing near. These words of the Lord Jesus, as recorded in Luke 21:28, are further affirmed in Mark 37:13, where we see His command: "What I say to one, I say unto all; watch."

Therefore, in the spirit of "watching," we must consider what God's prophets tell us to watch for as the end of the age comes more and more into view. The Apostle Paul, in that regard, gave some specific features that will mark the end of the age:

For men shall be lovers of their own selves, covetous, boasters, proud, blasphemers, disobedient to parents, unthankful, unholy,

13

Without natural affection, trucebreakers, false accusers, incontinent, fierce, despisers of those that are good,

Traitors, heady, highminded, lovers of pleasures more than lovers of God;

Having a form of godliness, but denying the power thereof: from such turn away. (2 Timothy 3:2–5)

I often refer to these indicators as the characteristics of end-times people. In describing these signals, Paul puts them within a period he calls "perilous times": "This know also, that in the last days perilous times shall come" (2 Timothy 3:1). Let's look now at the very first of the traits he lists: "lovers of their own selves." As I said, it will be more than enough to get me into some trouble, most likely.

I say that because I believe the most popular thing in our culture in America today is involved directly in this condemning characteristic. The younger adult generations—from the Millennials born in the 1980s and 1990s through Gen Z-ers born since that time—are the most into exhibiting this quality, but they are by no means the only segment of the culture involved. A former president of the United States, for example, engaged in this behavior on a number of occasions, as gleefully reported by his fawning press—and by that I mean most all of the mainstream news and entertainment media.

I'm talking, of course, about the selfie. The selfie, if I really need to define it, is a photograph taken of one's self with one's cell phone. The image then is shared through social networks to enhance the self-image and desired celebrity the individual wants to present to the world. The selfie is but the tip of the proverbial iceberg in revealing this end-times characteristic. The bulk of that iceberg is made up of the vast social-networking services such as Facebook, Instagram, Twitter, and the most-recently launched Threads platform.

See, I told you I would be in trouble—probably with you, the reader. I know my view of this is just reaching for application of the Apostle Paul's perilous-times condemnation, in the opinion of many. I still believe this is a primary indicator of where we are on God's prophetic timeline. People are increasingly becoming "lovers of their own selves," and they are demonstrating that "self-love" via countless shared photos and reels.

It might seem like an innocuous charge—even a silly one. But, I think it is much more relevant than any of us can imagine.

In my 2016 book, *Rapture Ready…or Not: 15 Reasons This Is the Generation That Will Be Left Behind*, I point to the serious ramifications such self-love is producing as Christ's call to His Church in the Rapture nears. Here is an excerpt from that part of the book:

> Psychologists and sociologists have for years planted in the minds of Americans that self-esteem is something that is important to making a successful life. These point to the fact that at the center of most every problem of the human condition resides the feelings of inadequacy and self-loathing.
>
> We are told that the radical Islamists who attacked on September 11, 2001, did so because they felt inferior due to US treatment that looked down upon them. The whole matter involving the attacks that took the lives of more than three thousand that day, therefore, convinced those in charge of the US State Department to employ a study group designed to help determine how to make those who hate us, particularly in the Middle East, no longer hate us.
>
> So ingrained is self-love in our nation that we in delusion covet the admiration of those who hate us with satanic rage born out of our support for Israel, not out of envy and low self-esteem on the terrorists' part.
>
> The terrorists, murderers, gang members, rapists, and all other of those who commit crimes these days are analyzed by the woolly-minded psychologists and sociologists based upon the

premise that the perpetrators hate themselves, thus all others who they see as deserving of their victimization.

God's Word says, "For no man ever yet hated his own flesh" (Ephesians 5:29a). In other words, self-loathing is not part of our DNA. Quite the opposite is true. The Bible says those who don't have the Holy Spirit are of their father, the devil. Satan is the ultimate example of self-love.

The social engineers tell us the secret to ultimately producing a healthy cultural environment is high self-esteem. A sense of self-worth will make us live up to our own great expectations.

Rather than love of self, however, God's Word tells us to love others, to esteem others more than ourselves, to humble ourselves before God. This generation is obviously doing none of these.[3]

That we are in perilous times can't be denied, except by the most willfully uncomprehending. I'm afraid many device-wielding people of this "Selfie Generation" fit within the universe of those destined to be left behind when Christ calls the Church in the Rapture.

We are very near that time. The evidence is flashing in every direction we look. We must lift up Christ at every opportunity so many will come to Jesus for salvation when the Holy Spirit draws them to the Savior.

Form of Godliness but Denying Its Power

At the end of his list of the characteristics of end-times man as recorded in 2 Timothy 3, Paul says people will have a "form of godliness," but will "deny the power thereof." Nowhere does Jesus, Paul, or any other of the prophets tell of a time when people will be turning to the Gospel message en masse for the salvation of their souls.

However, when I was recently scrolling through my TV channels, I heard more than one preacher say we are to get ready for the "anointing" in these last days. The "anointing" to which they referred, I found out by listening further, meant the speakers believed a special ability will be placed upon all within the Body of Christ. The "anointing" will bring about a great revival and massive move of the Holy Spirit that will bring a tremendous number of souls to salvation.

The preachers I heard didn't say where in the Bible this promised anointing is found. At least I missed it if they did. And that's the problem I have with this last-days, great revival I've heard about for years. I can't find a scriptural proof-text that makes such a promise.

There are references that many people will be saved during the Tribulation. For example, Revelation 7:9–17 foretells a time when a tremendous multitude of saints alongside the angelic billions will bow before the throne of God. John the Revelator is told these are the martyrs who came out of the Great Tribulation. God will wipe away all their tears and comfort them forever in his majestic presence.

There are other references to a multitude of souls being added to God's Kingdom. All of those references, however, point to the time *following* the Church Age. I can find no specific prophecy that there will be either a great end-of-this-age revival or of a massive number of souls being added to the Kingdom because of such a revival.

I'm not saying that a revival and an addition to the Kingdom of the magnitude these preachers proclaim can't happen; I'm just saying that if it does, it hasn't been prophesied anywhere in Scripture that I can find.

On the other hand, there are prophecies of the times leading up to the Tribulation that tell quite a different story than the prediction of a last-days revival. Jesus, Himself, said "the love of many will grow cold." People will be like they were in the days of Noah and of Lot; they will be doing evil and thinking only evil thoughts while the business of daily life goes on as usual.

The Apostle Paul says "evil men and seducers will grow worse and worse, deceiving and being deceived," and that even within the Church, people will be falling for false teachers and devilish doctrines. Not only will these folks be following "strange winds of doctrine," but they will "heap to themselves teachers, having itching ears."

In other words, they won't endure sound doctrine, but will follow fables. Much of this very thing is going on in the world of Christendom even as I write this.

John implies that, in the last days, the "spirit of Antichrist," not the Holy Spirit, will dominate the human condition. Here is what he writes:

Little children, it is the last time: and as ye have heard that antichrist shall come, even now are there many antichrists; whereby we know that it is the last time. (1 John 2:18)

Who is a liar but he that denieth that Jesus is the Christ? He is antichrist, that denieth the Father and the Son. (1 John 2:22)

And every spirit that confesseth not that Jesus Christ is come in the flesh is not of God: and this is that [spirit] of antichrist, whereof ye have heard that it should come; and even now already is it in the world. (1 John 4:3)

For many deceivers are entered into the world, who confess not that Jesus Christ is come in the flesh. This is a deceiver and an antichrist. (2 John 1:7)

Many of the largest church assemblies today fit the portrayal of the Laodicean church addressed in Revelation 3:14–22. These most dramatically manifest the Antichrist spirit through their 1) turning more and more toward universalism and 2) embracing replacement theology.

Universalism is the burgeoning belief system that teaches that there are many ways to God the Father and Heaven. It is a direct turning away from Jesus Christ as the only Way, Truth, and Life (John 14:6).

Replacement theology is the satanic lie accepted by more and more so-called mainstream Christian ministries that hold that the Church has replaced Israel as recipient of God's promises to Abraham, Isaac, and Jacob. This, of course, is a massive part of the very satanic ploy that will ultimately bring all peoples of the earth to Armageddon.

We don't have to hear of ABC's *The View* host Joy Behar mocking Vice President Mike Pence's Christian faith to know the spirit of Antichrist is surging. Mocking anything and everything to do with the name of Jesus Christ is rampant, even within a large percentage of those who claim Christianity as their spiritual platform. One great example of this is Catholic Pope Francis, who has a number of times proclaimed there is more than one way to Heaven.

This is a blatant display of the Antichrist spirit surging in these closing moments of the Age of Grace.

Jesus Describes Perilous Times

Paul's prophetic words about perilous times to come are inspired by the One who is the Word. Jesus is the true author of the Bible (John 1:1).

So when we read words issued straight from the Lord's own mouth, they have special significance. No one but God knows the end from the beginning. His Word proves that again and again. What Jesus says about things to come is profoundly important to read and heed.

With that in mind, let's consider Jesus' words about the last-days perilous times as juxtaposed against the issues and events taking place around us that so often "vex" us, as Lot, the believer of ancient times who lived in Sodom, might have put it.

Jesus, when His disciples asked about the signs of His Second Coming, said:

> Then said he unto them, Nation shall rise against nation, and king-
> dom against kingdom: And great earthquakes shall be in divers

places, and famines, and pestilences; and fearful sights and great signs shall there be from heaven. (Luke 21:10–11)

In other places, the Lord described these signs as coming upon the earth in birth-pang-like convulsions. There would be an increase in frequency and intensity of these issues and events.

One of the key indicators for us to look at in Christ's prophecy is the term "nation against nation." The Greek word for "nation" in this case is *ethnos*. Jesus was describing a time in the future when there would be a tremendous rise in the number of ethnic conflicts. This is one of the key descriptions of our times.

We have to look no farther than our own nation to determine that we're in ethnic turmoil. It is contrived disorder, foisted upon us by globalists who want to move America into a one-world configuration.

Black Lives Matter and Antifa are proven to be groups organized and funded by the likes of George Soros, a Hungarian-American businessman dedicated to creating a global order. These organizations have ginned up the ever-intensifying rage of rebellious anarchists within those who harbor racial hatred that has literally brought American cities to ruin societally, culturally, and, most assuredly, economically.

In my view, the 2020 COVID-19 outbreak continues to be used by the globalists as a bludgeon against America's people. The powers and principalities of Ephesians 6:12 are fomenting this nation-against-nation, end-of-the-age conflict.

This brings together the "ethnic hatreds" and "pestilence" terms in Jesus' prophecy. The evil Jesus warned of is intentional intensification of these perilous times. Although COVID and its proliferating strains are a contrived pestilence, it is pestilence nonetheless. It is a precursor to the great, *real* pandemics that will kill millions during the Tribulation era. What we've been seeing over the past few years is implementation of a control mechanism laying groundwork for the coming Antichrist regime to use.

Jesus described precisely the racial hatred that would prevail just before He returns to put an end to this wicked rebellion. We will look at this prophecy again throughout this book. God's Word warns about this evil and its fatal destiny in Psalm 2:

> The kings of the earth set themselves, and the rulers take counsel together, against the LORD, and against his anointed, saying, Let us break their bands asunder, and cast away their cords from us. He that sitteth in the heavens shall laugh: the Lord shall have them in derision. Then shall he speak unto them in his wrath, and vex them in his sore displeasure. (Psalm 2:2–5)

Jesus stated further:

> And there shall be signs in the sun, and in the moon, and in the stars; and upon the earth distress of nations, with perplexity; the sea and the waves roaring. (Luke 21:25)

Although a case can easily be made for astonishing evidence of things going on in space that have people looking into that dark vastness for answers, it is the second part of this prophecy that is profoundly relevant to this time so near the end of the Age of Grace.

Economic turmoil caused by the worldwide COVID lockdowns has had the nations during these perilous times "in distress," with great and growing "perplexity." Great Britain, France, Australia, and other major Western economies are experiencing conditions like those described by the Lord.

America, the nation to whose dollar most all the world is intricately linked, is but one event or occurrence away from total collapse. Although our government and the mainstream media won't confess this to the American people or the world that depends on the dollar, that collapse could come at any moment, many who are in the know fear.

Some perhaps not so much in the know, in terms of economic acumen (yours truly, for example), understand that the moment that will break the proverbial camel's back is about to occur.

I write, of course, about the Rapture of all believers in Jesus Christ. Jesus' words point toward that moment of removal from the Tribulation that will follow that great event:

And when these things begin to come to pass, then look up, and lift up your heads; for your redemption draweth nigh. (Luke 21:28)

2

$\circ\!\!\!\!\sim$

Sodom-like Society

WE WHO LOOK INTO BIBLE PROPHECY and try to understand things taking place that might have prophetic significance are often accused of approaching all this through an *Amerocentric* prism. That is, we concentrate too much on how God's Word might apply to America.

If we do this—and I concede that we do in much of our analysis—we look through this prism because America, as a nation, is so obviously guilty before God. This nation is the most materially blessed in all of human history. It is also one of the most spiritually blessed, in that the nation was founded on Judeo-Christian principles by men who, if not Christian, at least chose to tether our founding to the unmovable pillars of biblical morality and reverence for human life.

Yet, at the present, there is a movement into wickedness that rivals that in ancient Sodom. With all the evil taking place, while it's business as usual on the surface of society and culture, the finger of guilt must, like when Daniel read the handwriting on the wall before the drunken group of Babylonians (see Daniel chapter 5), even now be indicating the nation has been weighed in the balance and found wanting.

I say America is "guilty" because it takes a very quick look into a mirror to see that we've strayed about as far as possible from biblical precepts for conduct of life.

I've looked at the Greek word *apostasia* lately and believe this term, found in 2 Thessalonians chapter 2, might be both: 1) a spatial or physical departure; and 2) a spiritual or defection-from-faith departure.

Let no man deceive you by any means: for that day shall not come, except there come a falling away [apostasia] first, and that man of sin be revealed, the son of perdition. (2 Thessalonians 2:3)

While I continue to believe *apostasia* means "spatial departure," certainly students of Bible prophecy can't help but conclude that a profound *apostasia*, or spiritual departure, has taken place in this highly blessed nation. It is to an extent that those who profess Christ have, it can be asserted, defected from the faith, thus weakened resistance to the onslaught of Sodom-like evil.

We can look to American society and culture in general to determine whether it is true that there has been a profound departure from the faith—spiritual *apostasia*. People who do not know Jesus Christ as Savior are in the great majority. These have not "fallen away," as prophesied in the 2 Thessalonians chapter 2 passage above. They can't "fall away," because they've never been in the "salvation" category to begin with; people can't fall from a position they've never occupied. The only way to "fall away" is to have once been in that higher position.

Now, let's not get confused. We aren't talking about losing one's salvation. Nothing and nobody can snatch believers from God's mighty hand once they have experienced salvation through belief in the Lord Jesus Christ—God's only way to redemption and Heaven for eternity. (Read John 14: 6 and Romans 8:38–39.)

Apostasia, in the spiritual sense of falling away, involves those who have *falsely professed Christ as Savior*—who have put their faith only in the system of Christianity, but not in Christ, Himself, for salvation. They have never truly believed in God's one and only way to Himself in the redemption process.

So, in the spiritual sense, America is likely the most notable nation of this last-days falling away or *apostasia*. America has the largest number of *professing* adherents to the *system* called Christendom, but those aren't necessarily a part of the true Christian faith. The question, then, is do we see a movement away from true Christianity? The following gives a resounding answer:

NAPLES, Florida (LifeSiteNews) – A "Christian" church in Florida plans to host on Saturday an LGBTQ "Youth Pride Conference," featuring a drag show and a "sex education" talk by a Planned Parenthood speaker.

The event, which is being run by the Gay, Lesbian and Straight Education Network (GLSEN), is advertised as "an exploration of LGBTQ issues facing today's youth," "organized by and for LGBTQ students."

The host church, the Naples United Church of Christ (Naples UCC), styles itself as a "progressive church in terms of openness to a wide theological spectrum and the wide variety of lifestyles and orientations in our culture."

In addition to a drag show featuring "local drag queens," the event will hold a variety of talks during breakout sessions, with themes including "Forbidden Queer Literature," "Inclusive Sex Education," with Kathryn Ross, who works for Planned Parenthood, "Coming Out," and "Navigating a Religious Identity."[4]

My friend Dr. David Reagan, founder of Lamb and Lion Ministries and *Christ in Prophecy* television programs, provides troubling facts we must face about America falling away from that Christianity and becoming more and more Sodom-like, thus positioned for divine judgment. He wrote the following in 2012. Things have only gotten worse since that time:

Think about it. Since 1973, we have murdered our babies in their mothers' wombs at the rate of 4,000 a day, totaling nearly 60 million, and their blood cries out for vengeance.

We consume more than one-half of all the illegal drugs produced in the world, yet we constitute only 5% of the world's population.

We spend $2.8 billion dollars per year on Internet pornography, which is more than half the world total of $4.9 billion.

Our rate of cohabiting partners has increased tenfold since 1960, totaling over 12 million unmarried partners today.

Our divorce rate is the highest of any nation in the world.

Forty percent of our children are born to unmarried women.

We spend over $100 billion per year on gambling.

Our number one drug problem is alcohol, producing over 17.6 million adults who are alcoholics or who have alcohol problems.

Our nation has become a debt junkie, leading the world in both government debt and personal debt.

Blasphemy of God's name, His Word, and His Son has become commonplace in our media.

We are the moral polluter of planet earth through the distribution of our immoral, violent and blasphemous television programs and movies.

We have forsaken the nation of Israel, demanding that they surrender their heartland and divide their capital city.

We have become a nation that calls good evil and evil good. And we are paying the price:

Our schools have become arenas of deadly violence.

Our prison population is increasing exponentially, from 500,000 in 1980 to over 2.5 million today. Over 7.2 million of our people are under some form of correctional supervision.

Over 1.5 million of our women are reported victims of domestic violence each year, and it is estimated that the majority of cases are never reported.

We are currently averaging over 3 million child abuse cases each year, involving 6 million children.

We experience more than 12 million crimes every year, more than any other nation in the world.

Teen violence has increased exponentially, with youngsters killing each other over tennis shoes.

Gangs are terrorizing our cities.

Even the nicest of our neighborhoods are no longer safe, requiring us to protect our homes with security systems and weapons.

Our money is becoming increasingly worthless.

Our economy is being choked to death by a pile of debt that is beyond comprehension.

Our major corporations and labor unions are in bondage to greed.

Our society has become deeply divided, splintered among competing groups defined by racial, religious and economic factors.

Our families are being destroyed by an epidemic of divorce.

Our entertainment industry consists of vulgarians amusing barbarians.

One of our fastest growing businesses is the pagan practice of tattooing and body piercing.

Our universities and media outlets are controlled by radical leftists who hold God in contempt.

Our federal government has become top-heavy with bureaucrats who are insensitive to taxpayers.

Our politicians have become more concerned with power than service.

All levels of government have become increasingly oppressive, seeking to regulate every aspect of our lives.

Taxation has become confiscatory in nature.

Our legal system has been hijacked by activists who desire to impose their will on the people, regardless of what the people desire.

Our freedom of speech is being threatened by "hate crime" legislation.

Our forms of sports are becoming increasingly violent, reminiscent of the gladiators of ancient Rome.

Our society has become star-stuck, more interested in celebrities than people of integrity.

Our churches are caught up in an epidemic of apostasy as they set aside the Word of God in an effort to cozy up to the world and gain its approval.

We are experiencing one major natural disaster after another in unprecedented volume and ferocity.

We have become afflicted with a plague of sexual perversion, producing an army of hard core militant homosexuals.

In summary, we are a people who have become desensitized to sin, and in the process, we have forgotten how to blush.[5]

America has, it would seem, been chosen in a way by God for special purposes, including to be the physical protector of Israel during its rebirth and to the end of this age. Therefore, America has been blessed by the Almighty, from her own birth, with founding fathers who held to godly precepts.

No other nation has been more steeped in the Christian faith than the United States. Therefore, the Amerocentric view in consideration of whether we can see spiritual defection or *apostasia* in this time so near the end of the Age of Grace (Church Age) is relevant and even essential.

That America is becoming the modern-day Sodom cannot be missed. It's sad to consider that our nation might have already lost God's blessings, but we must reflect on that possibility.

We can, individually, continue to receive our God's blessings by remaining faithful in every way to His high calling—to look to Jesus Christ with all our praise and look to Him to guide our pathways.

Above all, we must do our utmost to avoid the mistakes of the people God condemns, no matter the generation. We see that condemnation in His words through the prophet Jeremiah:

Were they ashamed when they had committed abomination? nay, they were not at all ashamed, neither could they blush: therefore shall they fall among them that fall: in the time of their visitation they shall be cast down, saith the Lord. (Jeremiah 8:12)

Sounding of Sirens

When that funny, irritating noise coming from your TV set goes off, what is your reaction? I'm talking about the grating sound that disrupts the program you're watching or happen to have on while you do other things.

The noise is followed by an announcement: "This is a test. This is only a test. If this had been an actual emergency..." Well, you know what I'm talking about.

When that goes off, I must admit my first, instantaneous thought is still: *Could it be a nuclear attack?*

This automatic reaction comes, I have little doubt, from the time of "duck and cover!"—the instruction that dominated my days as a kid. We were told that if the sirens started announcing a nuclear attack, we should get under our desks if we were at school. We were to jump off our bikes and try to get under something, lie flat in a ditch, or hide behind anything available if we were out and about.

I've mentioned before that when I was a sophomore in high school, rumor had it that atomic war with the Soviets would happen on a certain Friday. It caused angst for some, but not everyone paid any attention to the rumor or the warnings to duck and cover. I guess I've always been a bit geopolitically sensitive.

So it was that I tried to imagine what the people of Hawaii must have experienced several years ago when their devices and televisions announced incoming nuclear missiles. It wasn't a test; everyone was instructed to seek immediate shelter.

There was crying and gnashing of teeth, to use biblical language. People got under mattresses with their families or boarded themselves up in garages. One grandfather herded his grandchildren into a sewer manhole. It was a time of anxiety far beyond anything I've ever experienced.

If an actual nuke had been headed to the beautiful islands of Hawaii, no beauty would remain following the impact. It's almost but not impossible to imagine what that part of the islands would have looked like, because we have the films of the Hiroshima and Nagasaki atomic bombs to graphically remind us of the results of such weaponry. We have the films of the Bikini tests in the 1950s that demonstrated the horrific destructiveness of nuclear devices far more powerful than the bombs used on Japan to end the war.

Thankfully, the feared attack on Hawaii was a false alarm. The people under the mattresses, in their garages, and in the manholes could emerge to consider how things could have ended so differently. We can hope the accidental siren alert of those years ago will be a wake-up call letting everyone know just how quickly (less than twelve minutes from time of the alert) such devastation can come upon us.

Devastation is coming that has a much, much quicker time of arrival than ten to twelve minutes upon totally unsuspecting people. There will be no alarm to warn those under this incoming destruction. That is, no annoying sounds will disrupt TV programs or announce on various devices what is about to occur.

However, the siren has been blaring, warning that the catastrophic impact is about to take place. As a matter of fact, I and a number of others have been sounding the alarm for some time. The wreckage will far surpass what that nuclear-tipped missile would have caused, had it been an actual attack. This imminent, catastrophic event will result in as many as three-fourths of people on earth perishing over a period of seven years.

Those upon whom this calamity is about to fall are oblivious to warning. Many don't even believe the impending disaster is a prophetic fact. They make fun of the notion. I'm referring, of course, to preachers who claim to follow Jesus Christ, but don't believe He will return in a cataclysmic way to the earth.

These, if they have any opinion or care one way or the other, believe Christ will return and take over for the Church. The Church, they believe, will have made worthy His Kingdom, over which He will then reign.

Only that's not what the Bible says. The Revelation 19:11 return is to a war-torn planet where most of its inhabitants have died in the violence and wrath of seven years of Tribulation.

Many of these types of theologians say they don't believe the book of Revelation even belongs in the canon of Scripture. There is, they say, no Rapture—no time of great trouble under the rule of someone known as Antichrist. That stuff is all to somehow be taken in a spiritual way, not literally.

Jesus will indeed come back to rule and reign over a planet that is much like it was in the time of Eden before the Fall. But, He—not the theologians who think they will prepare the way for Heaven on earth—will do the restoration. When Christ calls all believers to Himself at the Rapture, that very moment, devastation will begin to fall. It will be just like in the time of Lot when he was removed from Sodom (read Luke 17:26–30).

So, the siren of Bible prophecy is unheard by the vast majority of humanity. But, it is ringing more loudly every day in the ears of those who are spiritually attuned. That's why we present these books and articles. We want to broadcast that a devastating time is coming—and at any moment.

One signal is most prominent. Israel is being forced by Satan's globalist minions to give in to demands to further divide God's land. The Lord is on the cusp of taking the Church home with Him. He will then again begin dealing with His beloved Israel. It will be a time of His wrath while He purges rebellious earth-dwellers and rescues for Himself a people to populate the millennial earth.

The sirens are sounding!

3

Generation of "Evil Men and Seducers"

THERE'S PERHAPS NO PROFOUNDER INDICATOR of where this generation stands on God's prophetic timeline than the most pervasive ingredient of the spirit of the age. Jesus pointed to this as a specific signal believers are to be aware of when all other signs of His return to earth are in view.

> And as he sat upon the Mount of Olives, the disciples came unto him privately, saying, "Tell us, when shall these things be? and what shall be the sign of thy coming, and of the end of the world?" And Jesus answered and said unto them, "Take heed that no man deceive you." (Matthew 24:3–4)

Paul the apostle spoke of this same ingredient that would permeate the general timeframe of Christ's return:

> But evil men and seducers shall wax worse and worse, deceiving, and being deceived. (2 Timothy 3:13)

The spirit of this wicked age drips with the satanic venom of deception. It is the same venom injected into humankind in the Garden of Eden when the serpent seduced Eve, then caused Adam to believe the lie that he and Eve could be like God. Through today's zeitgeist (spirit of the age) flows the same toxic, Luciferian evil.

Evil men and seducers assault our eyes and ears every waking moment. Our culture is saturated with deceit at every level. The lies have become so blatant they've numbed our senses as a generation, in many cases.

For example, many can now be told—and believe, in some cases— that a man can become a woman, a girl can become a boy, men can become pregnant, and it's no longer wrong for adults to engage in sexual acts with children.

As a matter of fact, the *woke,* reprobate minds that are the thought police tell us we can no longer call adults who would sexually relate to children in the most wicked ways "pedophiles." They must now be treated as normal and called "minor-attracted persons (MAPs)." And there is less and less pushback to such monstrous, upside-down thinking.

The deception infects the very souls of humankind with a lie like the one the serpent whispered to Eve: "Yea, hath God said?" Satan thus is, during this time so near the end of the age, blatantly, through the woke insanity of his human minions, telling all who will listen that God's order of creation is all wrong. We can be our own god. We can be other than the gender in which we were born. God is wrong. People can do what is right in their own eyes.

We're lied to at every juncture by the government that was once said by Abraham Lincoln and the Constitution to be the government of, by, and for the people. In politics and through bureaucratic manipulations, the reprobate mindset of Romans 1:28 is in full bloom.

Proliferate spending has, in effect, bankrupted the US. Once elected to office, those who find themselves in charge of the tax dollars of the American people too often embrace the lobbying minions and their desire to increase their wealth and influence rather than tend to the fiscal responsibility they owe the voters who put them in office. They feather their own nests by selling their influence.

As a result, over the years, we've come to a national debt that can never be resolved.

And now it appears that the wicked leadership of the nation—and of the entire world that America's dollar base influences—is intent on going to a digital form of currency to somehow reset the economic fiasco they've created through electronic manipulation. This, as some (including me) view it, is actually a ruse implemented by the father of lies. Satan, through his reprobate, evil genius, is maneuvering his human-governing underlings to set the stage by instituting electronic funds and the digital way of doing business for the Antichrist system of buying and selling through the 666, numbers-and-marks model of Revelation 13:16–18.

Evil men and seducers are ramping up efforts to bring America down so the global order they want to build—the New World Order—can proceed.

The deceit to get that process underway in earnest can be understood through the so-called pandemic America and the world recently endured. More and more, it all looks to be a great lie designed to bring about Satan's coming man of sin and his regime of tyranny and the Tribulation.

My friend Daymond Duck recently touched on this deception:

Concerning deceit in the US government and tracking every-one: on Feb. 28, 2023, in testimony before a House Select Subcommittee, Dr. Marty Makary, professor at the Johns Hopkins School of Medicine, said, "The greatest perpetrator of misinformation during the [COVID] pandemic was the US government."

Makary cited a long list of government false statements, an authoritative study that refuted some of them, experts that refuted some of them, and the report noted that the release of Twitter Files verifies that the US government deliberately tried to silence experts on many of the issues.

It is important to understand that the government that was perpetrating false information wants to keep records on every US citizen and control their life.[6]

The great deception by evil men and seducers points to things of monumental importance:

1) The seven-year Tribulation is on the cusp of engulfing this world of rebels against the God of Heaven.

2) Jesus Christ, the King of all kings, is readying to return and throw down Satan's false Christ and his wicked kingdom.

3) The Rapture can (and, we are believing, *will*) very soon take Christians out of harm's way so we will be with the Lord forever.

Today when we look around the world and the way things have moved from a "saner" time until now, those who care to consider these matters see an increasingly wicked world. Such observers see, for example, Russia and Vladimir Putin, China and Xi Jinping, and North Korea and Kim Jong Un. These are leaders who hold their populations under absolute control, sometimes with the greatest cruelty imaginable.

Sadly, few observers care to gauge the wickedness we face as a world while things are sucked into the gravity of the increasingly evil times. As a result, America, under the greatest, most noble experiment in human government, now faces insanity that threatens tyranny equal to the despotism of some of the most terrible regimes ever. This is, of course, in keeping with God's prophetic Word for the wrap-up of history.

Many, including myself, considered in times past that the Antichrist system of control would *suddenly* leap onto the scene once the Rapture occurred. The call of Christians into the air would be what set in motion that sucking of left-behind humankind into the gravity of what would almost instantly become Tribulation tyranny.

Some warned of incrementalism—the slow changes through Luciferian incursion into the human condition. But none foresaw the almost instantaneous dive into the reprobate sea of debauchery into which many have plunged during this late hour.

Freedom found in God's prescription for humankind has been abandoned to the upside-down madness that separates folks farther and farther from the Creator who knows best for us. And it's not just the Putins, the Xis, and Kims who are the evil men and seducers. We, in this once-great republic, now face some of the vilest and most seductive forces on earth. Determined to bring down not only America, but all vestiges of the Christian faith, they're making inroads by changing what Christianity means.

I found the following think-piece most interesting in considering this force of evil men and seducers:

In a recent Front Page column, Dennis Prager criticizes the idea that people are basically good. The belief that humans are inherently good is both "foolish" and "dangerous," writes Prager, and it leads to much suffering. He offers several sobering examples from recent history of what happens to people who put their trust in human nature.

Prager was prompted to write his rebuttal when a respected Jewish publication published an article by an Orthodox rabbi claiming that "Judaism posits that people are basically good." The idea has long been prevalent among non-Orthodox rabbis, but Prager was surprised that an Orthodox Jew would subscribe to an idea that is clearly rejected in the Torah.

The notion that human nature is basically good is also rejected in the rest of the Bible—and just as strongly in the New Testament as in the Old. Which brings me to my main point. Over the last six decades, belief in human goodness has become an article of faith for many Christians as well as for Jews.

This is particularly true of many mainstream Protestants and Roman Catholics. For the Catholic Church, the belief has served as a wrecking ball. Numerous polls have shown a massive decline in church attendance among Catholics (and other Christians), and a corresponding drop in the number who identify as Christians.

Different people give different reasons for the decline of Christian belief, but for me the obvious reason is that Christians have replaced the idea of human sinfulness with the idea of human goodness. And when you do that, you undercut the whole rationale for Christianity—namely, that we are sinners in need of redemption. If human beings are good the way they are, then there is no need for a Savior to free us from our sins.[7]

The founding fathers of the United States recognized the depravity of humans. The idea that we are good flies in the face of God's truth: "There is none good, no not one" (see Romans 3:10).

Unless people are willing to admit they are not good and need a Savior to save them from their sinfulness, there is no hope. This is the great, seductive ploy of the devil, and has been since he tempted Eve in the Garden. "Ye shall be as God," he seduced and beguiled. The ploy is working more effectively now than ever, and we see the results with so many turning their backs on God, doing what is right in their own eyes in preparation for the time of God's wrath and judgment. We are now at the Romans 1:28 place at the very end of the age when great numbers of the world's population have been given over to a reprobate mind.

Good is now called evil and evil good. Thankfully, God still invites individuals to salvation, but we continue en masse down that broad way to destruction. However, there is a narrow gate, Jesus said, that leads to eternity with the Father. Jesus is that narrow gate. Don't listen to the evil men and seducers of these increasingly sin-darkened days.

"Evil Men and Seducers" in Public Education

There is no dearth of information to address the Apostle Paul's prophecy about "evil men and seducers" for the time so near the end of the Age of Grace. We now have in our once biblically influenced nation an entire public education system steeped in every sort of wickedness. And it begins at the most basic level.

Kindergarteners are now exposed to the likes of drag queens and their perversions. Grades above that level are routinely taught the anti-God lessons of transgender and critical race theory (CRT) and are inculcated on a regular basis that America as founded and over the years has been a tyrannical, colonial master of peoples around the world.

History is revised—and in many cases, it is completely rewritten—to make textbooks present fabrications and outright lies. Marxist socialism and even worse are foisted upon the students of secondary education, and, particularly, upon those enrolled in colleges and universities.

Anti-God educators count human life itself as a problem: Mother Earth suffers because human beings are destroying her, thus abortion is preferred to bringing, in particular, the dark-skinned races to birth. (More than 40 percent of the millions of babies murdered in their mothers' wombs by the likes of Planned Parenthood are Black.)

Several generations have been seduced to believe heterosexuality and homosexuality are equally acceptable within cultural and societal norms. As a matter of fact, anyone who adheres to the previous, traditional views of the matters involved are now deemed to be, at best, homophobic bigots worthy of being publicly ostracized at every turn, and at worst mentally ill. Homosexuality itself, of course, was a thing psychologists and psychiatrists, in more rational, past times, pointed to as aberrant behavior or mental instability.

"Evil Men and Seducers" in Science

Now evil men who propose creating transhumanism (superhuman/ technology hybrids produced by science) have emerged and are in the process of seducing all of humanity in anti-God ways even more egregious than those that have been inflicted by anti-God, anti-American educators since the 1960s. These exhibit the earmarks of influence of the demonic realm. Ephesians 6:12 is in view as never before:

> For we wrestle not against flesh and blood, but against princi-
> palities, against powers, against the rulers of the darkness of this
> world, against spiritual wickedness in high places.

This end-times manifestation of "evil men and seducers" is illustrated by the following:

One of the most enigmatic, sensational, and misguided thinkers of the last 10 years is Israeli historian and pop philosopher Yuval Noah Harari. His book *Sapiens*, published in English in 2015, sold over a million copies as it told the story of mankind's evolution. His 2017 book *Homo Deus* predicts a transhumanist future, a world where technology fundamentally reshapes what kind of entity human beings are.

"We humans should get used to the idea that we are no longer mysterious souls. We are now hackable animals," he told attendees at the 2020 World Economic Forum annual meeting. "By hacking organisms, elites may gain the power to reengineer the power of life itself," he said two years earlier. "This will be not just the greatest revolution in the history of humanity. This will be the greatest revolution in biology since the very beginning of life 4 billion years ago."

Harari's prophecy doesn't end there: "Science is replacing evolution by natural selection by evolution via intelligent design," he continued in 2018. "Not the intelligent design of some God above the clouds, but our intelligent design, and the intelligent design of our clouds: the IBM cloud, the Microsoft cloud...these are the new, driving forces of evolution.[8]

Yuval Noah Harari often issues blasphemous pronouncements that AI ventures are replacing the concept of the God of Heaven. Some even believe Harari to be Antichrist in the making. I don't believe that's the case, but he does exhibit the Antichrist spirit, to be sure. His work with the likes of Klaus Schwab, Bill Gates, and others within the World Economic Forum (WEF) does look to be a major platform that might produce the satanic regime headed by the man of sin, the son of perdition.

More Generational Traits

In chapter 1 of this book, we looked at a couple of the characteristics the Apostle Paul said would mark the generations living in the end time: being "lovers of their own selves" and "having a form of godliness, but denying the power thereof." Here, I'd like to circle back to look a little closer at some other of the traits listed in 2 Timothy: "without natural affection" (3:3), "false accusers" (3:3), and "heady, high-minded" (3:4).

"Without Natural Affection"

My own view of this category is that it refers in part, of course, to homosexuality and abortion. My wonderment has always been: How can anyone consider sexual relations with a person of the same sex as "natural" activity? How can anyone believe abortion to be "natural" in a mother dealing murderously with a baby in her womb? Yet these are two of the most prominent social and cultural indicators of our day.

In addition, we know from our news programs and feeds how "fierce" people can be in dealing with each other. That behavior certainly indicates "unnatural affection." News about brutality and criminal behavior seems to be the kind that most interests the viewing public—thus stimulates the news-reporting sources to broadcast it.

"False Accusers"

Now we come to the characteristic Paul terms "false accusers." This has, in my view, become the most evident of all in this particular hour while the end of the age draws to its conclusion.

The 2016 presidential election brought this one front and center for all to clearly discern. Any sound-thinking people can—if they simply open their eyes and ears—realize that the effort to destroy the forty-fifth president and his presidency has been the drive of the political left. As a matter of fact, I've deemed it as a satanic rage by both human and demonic minions that came against the Trump administration's efforts to get America back on track.

Certainly, America has been derailed, moving farther and farther away from God's directions for life on earth as put forth in His Holy Word. Having been founded on godly principles by the founding fathers, it has been Satan's plan to remove all tethers from those spiritual moorings. He has been phenomenally successful in doing so. The presidential administration that preceded Trump's and the deleterious achievements of that preceding president are proof of the fallen one's success in that regard.

The nefarious work of Satan and the minions continue through "false accusation." We will look briefly here at the most obvious.

I'm thinking about Christopher Steele, a former British intelligence agent who, for payment—apparently by the opposing candidate's campaign against Donald Trump—wrote a fictional dossier falsely accusing Trump of salacious activity while in a hotel room in Russia. This was done, it has been proven through many months and even years of closely examining the facts, to give the Foreign Intelligence Surveillance Act (FISA) judge reason to issue permission to open an investigation into Trump's collusion with Russia in the defeat of Hillary Clinton.

It was all totally false, of course, but special counsel Robert Mueller's investigation went on undeterred by facts. This is an example of *false accusation* for all the world to see.

No matter which channel or network that presented the news as it was unfolding, that was the number-one story. And, it has proven to be totally fake news. That, friends and countrymen, is "false accusers" doing their work right in our faces.

This particular characteristic of end-times man threatens to create a constitutional crisis, to tear apart the United States by dividing the nation in a way not even the Civil War could accomplish. The only comfort to those who are under the saving grace of the Lord Jesus Christ is that seeing all this in our headlines today means our redemption is drawing near.

"Heady, High-minded"

All we have to do is consider many of our congressional leaders and other governmental "servants"—such as those within our judicial system—to see the truth in Paul's condemning words about humankind being "heady" and "high-minded." These more often than not go against the will of the people in making decisions that rule, not serve, we the people.

Paul's prophecy is front and center as the world grows ever darker and evil men and seducers grow worse and worse. But this all means that we are to serve as God's light for those who do not accept Heaven's grace gift and who are doomed to suffer throughout the worst time of history.

These Days of Lot

LISTENING TO A TELEVISION NEWS REPORT one morning recently, I heard noise almost like a howling pack of wolves. (No longer able to see due to that aforementioned retinal disease-caused blindness, I "listen" to TV on occasion.)

I wondered what was going on to produce this strangely mixed combination of what sounded to be both humans and animals making unearthly noises. The racket went on and on with no commentary, so I continued to listen to find out the reason for the howling.

After about two minutes of the narrator-less noise, the reporter said it was a large group of Black Lives Matter (BLM) protesters. They were raving—and I do mean *raving*—against a black, formerly gay, Christian pastor who stood before them. There were so many bleeps deleting the expletives in the audio that they were almost continuous, with the raving disrupted to the point of not being able to make sense of what was being said by individual protestors. Among the mob was a large contingent of LGBTQ+ supporters.

The report then cut to the young preacher speaking with the reporter in a quiet setting following the confrontation. The pastor was explaining that he was now a Christian, a husband, and a father of two young children. He had been preaching in Chicago about what Christ had done for him in bringing him out of the homosexual lifestyle. He was completely free from that sinful life and was now sharing the word that Jesus is the answer to the group of folks he had formerly been a part of.

The preacher said he had received death threats and even had his home damaged; his relatives had been threatened to be burned along with their homes as well.

The TV report then went back to the video and audio with the lunatic-sounding raving that was full of bleeped-out profanity.

Many years ago, I heard a radio news report of a group of twenty-five or so members of a pro-homosexual organization surrounding a small San Francisco church. They weren't chanting, but in eerie, almost whispered tones, told what they planned to do in taking the children from the parents of the church parishioners and making them their own.

This was quickly dismissed as almost an aberration. It was unusual at that time, even for San Francisco. But today, that evil has grown into full-fledged threatening on the level of an infamous, ancient gathering in the now-disappeared city of Sodom. The account is found in Genesis 19.

Angelic visitors, in the form of men, came into Sodom and entered the home of Lot, the only man God found to be righteous—the only man who was a believer. The men of Sodom surrounded Lot's home and demanded that he send the visiting men out to them so they could "know" them. They were burning in their lust to have sexual relations with the strangers.

The following is God's Word on that time:

But before they lay down, the men of the city, even the men of Sodom, compassed the house round, both old and young, all the people from every quarter: And they called unto Lot, and said unto him, Where are the men which came in to thee this night? bring them out unto us, that we may know them. And Lot went out at the door unto them, and shut the door after him, and said, I pray you, brethren, do not so wickedly. (Genesis 19:4–7)

Lot's plea went unheeded. The homosexuals—and that must have been almost all of the males who were not younger children—said they would do worse to Lot than to the strangers if Lot didn't comply.

The story, of course, is that the angels blinded the would-be attackers.

It's interesting that the next thing to happen was Lot and his daughters were removed from the city, which was then completely decimated by God sending fire and brimstone. It is fascinating because Jesus said it will be just like that removal and judgment—just like in the "days of Lot" when He next is "revealed" (read again Luke 17:26—30).

This is the moment when Christ removes His Church from the planet in the Rapture. Jesus prophesied it would be just like that when He makes Himself known to the world in a cataclysmic way. Judgment will begin falling the very day He removes the Church, as it fell on Sodom and its sister city, Gomorrah, the day Lot and his daughters were removed from that wicked, judgment-destined area.

Evidence that society is quickly becoming like it was in the days of Lot is shown in reports like the following:

The San Francisco Gay Men's Chorus has released, and then deplatformed, a new video with a threat to many American parents:

"You think we're sinful, you fight against our right, you say we all lead lives you can't respect. But you're just frightened, you think that we'll corrupt your kids if our agenda goes unchecked. Fine, just this once, you're correct," the lyrics go.

"We'll convert your children, happens bit by bit, quietly and subtly and you will barely notice it, you can keep them from disco, warn about San Francisco, make them wear pleated pants, we don't care—

"We're coming for them, we're coming for your children! We're coming for them, we're coming for them, WE'RE COMING FOR YOUR CHILDREN!!!"...

"I guess it must be fun to fancy yourself a god!"

Explained the commentary, "Keep it up guys! You're doing great. There is nothing more unifying than telling people you are literally coming for their kids.

"Nothing!"

...[PJMedia stated,] "It seems the people who want to convert your children to their lifestyle and way of thinking don't even bother to hide it anymore. The so-called 'anti-racists' who peddle racist, anti-Western ideology say it out loud. They even have pet thug blackshirts to scare people into it. Antifa holds a summer camp to teach protest tactics to children. Men who wish to normalize pedophilia now call themselves 'minor-attracted persons' (they used to be NAMBLA) and pretend to fight for children's sexual freedom. Don't scoff, it's picking up traction."[9]

The raving, like howls of voracious wolves, can be heard across an increasingly, downward-spiraling society and culture. But, the Lord is still in complete control. His Restrainer is with us, so who can be against us?

And when you see all these things begin to come to pass, then look up and lift up your head, for your redemption draws near. (Luke 21:28)

Economic Boom on Track

Things are progressing swiftly in the area of economic rearrangements and derangements and those fiscal matters are tracking precisely on God's prophetic schedule. Because that timetable is unfolding in such dynamic fashion, I periodically offer a reminder of that prophetic progression.

Like in the case of all of my examination that has preceded these current financial considerations, my thoughts here aren't meant to applaud myself in any sense at all. They're to point out that this generation seems to be at the very place Jesus said the end-of-the-age generation will be at the time of the Rapture.

Every underlying indicator that this economy should have long ago imploded stares the experts in the face. Yet that bust has not occurred. As a matter of fact, those experts—that is, those with major media platforms—proclaim an unprecedented economic uptick. They broadcast from the proverbial rooftops that, despite some signs of recession worries, we can still count on the greatest economic trend in memory getting back on track.

Yet the lesser-known fiscal observers—many of whom are in the blogosphere—note that this perceived economic trend toward reaching unknown stratospherics is all built on nothing but faith in that not-undergirded financial structure—i.e., this supposed economic boom is built on nothing but air. It is like Wile E. Coyote, the cartoon character in "The Roadrunner Show," suspended in midair over a deep canyon. He just hangs there until, finally, gravity takes hold and he ends up in a puff of dust at the canyon's bottom.

Without intending to be sacrilegious or even slightly disrespectful toward the Lord's dealings with humankind, these times reflect something analogous to that 1966–1973 Saturday morning series. It seems the economic crash that should have already happened is suspended in midair. It's as if the tremendous weight of debt—the trillions of dollars that can never be repaid—is supernaturally made of non-effect. That is, the horrific weight just doesn't matter. The economic crash cannot take place because of some unseen force.

Economists who say a great crash is coming can't explain why it hasn't come already. They can only speculate it's because of sleight of hand by the wizards within the US Treasury and other high bastions of finance. But then they have to admit that no financial wizardry exists that could hold back such immense fiscal weight.

These, of course, don't see any such thing as something supernatural holding back a crash. Certainly, most would never attribute the holdup of that crash to the God of Heaven. Yet, they must acknowledge it is totally unprecedented and has unnatural elements running throughout the phenomenon.

And it is indeed a phenomenon. Never has there been such an extended time before economic correction takes place, according to the experts I've read and talked with. By now, these say, such an adjustment should have resulted in, at the very least, a relatively strong recession. Some believe a depression as catastrophic as the Great Depression of the 1930s should have taken place by now.

Now for the reason I mentioned at the beginning of this section that I in no way intend to pat myself on the back. At the end of 2010 and the beginning of 2011, I wrote a series of articles titled "Scanning a Fearful Future." My conclusion at the end of this ten-article series was that there would be no financial crash. Instead, I wrote there would be a financial uptick—even an era of economic boom. This was all based upon my consideration of whether this generation was reaching the time of Christ's intervention into the affairs of humankind. Specifically, I was pondering whether the Rapture of the Church was on the brink of taking place.

All of this, of course, was based upon Bible prophecy. It was predicted in the words of Jesus Christ, when He was on earth and teaching His disciples.

I expressed that I believed there would be no economic crash of the sort many emailers were writing me about with their fear that the US and the world were about to face Tribulation-like troubles. These problems, most message-senders feared, would have severe economic woes at their basis.

My contention remains that if we are as late in this dispensation of grace as I believe, there won't be time for all to come crashing down—economically and in other ways—then build positively again until the world reaches another time exactly like the current period. It would take many years, perhaps decades, to again come to where this generation finds itself, particularly in reference to America. And, America, despite harbingers to the contrary, is still the apex nation of the world in economic terms. If the US economy came crashing down, the entire world, so intricately linked to the almighty dollar, would suffer an even greater meltdown.

My conclusions are based upon Jesus' prophecy about the days of Noah and of Lot found in Matthew 24:36–42 and Luke 17:26–30. We've looked at these areas of Scripture already and will do so many more times throughout this volume.

Jesus said that rather than economic collapse, there would be a great uptick in buying, selling, building, and agricultural matters like planting, etc.

Since I first wrote about this subject in 2011, my findings have been validated. This, again, is because I believe God's Word on prophetic matters, not on my own soothsaying abilities or "word of knowledge."

America is in a financial downward trend at present, down from the uptick during the Trump days. The economic boom predicted by Jesus Christ is still on track; however; the nation has not yet defaulted, as feared by many experts.

The former president, Donald J. Trump, a builder of perhaps unprecedented ability, was, I'm convinced, supernaturally placed in a position to see to it that the economic status prophesied by the Lord Jesus has come to pass and remains in place for the wrap-up of the age. This is my contention that has, at least in my spirit, been wholeheartedly validated.

Records are still moving upward, despite erratic waves in the Dow and other economic sectors. This is despite that there is still the ominous trillions upon trillions of dollars of economic gravitational pull that should at any moment cause a catastrophic crash.

Jesus said such a crash will indeed take place, but at the moment He is next "revealed" to the world. That great event will be the Rapture, when His people—all those who have been saved through belief in His death, burial and resurrection—will be called to Heaven to be with Him for eternity (Revelation 4:2). Jesus said judgment would fall upon the rebels of planet earth that very day.

Jesus Christ is the only safe shelter from that coming, worldwide time of unprecedented horror. Again, Romans 10:9–10 is the way to make sure you are within His protective shelter during that great future storm.

Section II

Midnight Madness

5

Nearing Midnight and the
Doomsday Clock

JESUS SET HEAVEN'S END-TIMES CLOCK, foretelling when the second hand of eternity will reach near the midnight hour for the earth's inhabitants. He did so by giving God's heavenly family the assurance that we will be snatched up before that time; we will be rescued from this planet of rebels doomed to suffer His righteous wrath and judgment.

> And when these things begin to come to pass, then look up, and lift up your heads; for your redemption draweth nigh. (Luke 21:28)

The phrase "these things" in this verse refers to the issues and events of prophetic significance that have long since begun to "come to pass."

Todd Strandberg, founder of Raptureready.com, and I have for decades written commentaries on "these things" for the "Nearing Midnight" section of the Raptureready.com website. We have tried to show the progress toward that midnight hour. We've presented what we believe is not a "doomsday clock," but a marquee on the heavenly horizon announcing the great event that all who believe in Jesus Christ for salvation are swiftly approaching.

It is more than intriguing that, while we look at all the wickedness being done by the "evil men and seducers" who are growing "worse and worse," secular watchers of humankind's nearness to the same midnight hour perceive that time is almost up.

This came starkly into view with the most recent setting by the "Bulletin of the Atomic Scientist Doomsday Clock" watchdogs:

> A panel of international scientists has warned that humanity's continued existence is at greater risk than ever before, largely as a result of Russia's invasion of Ukraine.
>
> The *Bulletin of the Atomic Scientists* set its Doomsday Clock at 90 seconds to midnight, the closest to midnight the clock has been since it was established in 1947 to illustrate global existential threats at the dawn of the nuclear weapons age.
>
> Rachel Bronson, the president and CEO of the Bulletin, said the clock had been moved forward from 100 seconds to midnight, where it had been for the previous three years, "largely, though not exclusively, because of the mounting dangers in the war in Ukraine."
>
> "We are living in a time of unprecedented danger, and the Doomsday Clock time reflects that reality. Ninety seconds to midnight is the closest the clock has ever been set to midnight, and it's a decision our experts do not take lightly."[10]

Doomsday Clock

The Bulletin of the Atomic Scientists has told the world what time it is since 1947, when its famous clock appeared on the cover. Since then, the clock has moved forward and back, reflecting the state of international security.

The next page shows a timeline of doomsday clock settings that chronicle the clock-watchers' concerns throughout the years.

Doomsday Clock Table

YEAR	MINUTES UNTIL MIDNIGHT	SIGNIFICANT EVENT(S)
1947	7	The clock first appears on the Bulletin cover as a symbol of nuclear danger.
1949	3	The Soviet Union explodes its first atomic bomb.
1953	2	The United States and the Soviet Union test thermonuclear devices within nine months of one another.
1960	7	The clock moves in response to the growing public understanding that nuclear weapons made war between the major powers irrational. International scientific cooperation and efforts to aid poor nations are cited.
1963	12	The US and Soviet signing of the Partial Test Ban Treaty "provides the first tangible confirmation of what has been the Bulletin's conviction in recent years—that a new cohesive force has entered the interplay of forces shaping the fate of mankind."
1968	7	China acquires nuclear weapons; wars rage in the Middle East, the Indian subcontinent, and Vietnam; world military spending increases while development funds shrink.
1969	10	The US Senate ratifies the Nuclear Non-Proliferation Treaty.
1972	12	The United States and the Soviet Union sign the first Strategic Arms Limitation Treaty (SALT I) and the Anti-Ballistic Missile Treaty; progress toward SALT II is anticipated.
1974	9	SALT talks reach an impasse; India develops a nuclear weapon. "We find policy-makers on both sides increasingly ensnared, frustrated, and neutralized by domestic forces having a vested interest in the amassing of strategic forces."
1980	7	The deadlock in US-Soviet arms talks continues; nationalistic wars and terrorist actions increase; the gulf between rich and poor nations grows wider.
1981	4	Both superpowers develop more weapons for fighting a nuclear war. Terrorist actions, repression of human rights, and conflicts in Afghanistan, Poland, and South Africa add to world tension.
1984	3	The arms race accelerates. "Arms control negotiations have been reduced to a species of propaganda.... The blunt simplicities of force threaten to displace any other form of discourse between the superpowers."
1988	6	The United States and the Soviet Union sign a treaty to eliminate intermediate-range nuclear forces (INF); superpower relations improve; more nations actively oppose nuclear weapons.
1990	10	The clock, redesigned in 1989, reflects democratic movements in Eastern Europe, which shatter the myth of monolithic communism; the Cold War ends.
1991	17	The United States and the Soviet Union sign the long-stalled Strategic Arms Reduction Treaty (START) and announce further unilateral cuts in tactical and strategic nuclear weapons.
1995	14	Further arms reductions are stalled while global military spending continues at Cold War levels. Nuclear "leakage" from poorly guarded former Soviet facilities is recognized as a growing risk.
1998	9	India and Pakistan "go public" with nuclear tests. The United States and Russia can't agree on further deep reductions in their stockpiles.
2002	7	Little progress is made on global nuclear disarmament. The United States rejects a series of arms control treaties and announces it will withdraw from the Anti-Ballistic Missile Treaty. Terrorists seek to acquire and use nuclear and biological weapons.

Armageddon Clock

The Armageddon clock, unlike the doomsday clock, moves ever forward. Each tick of its second hand—the activity and status of the nation Israel and the issues and events of Bible prophecy—brings the world nearer the starting point of what will be humanity's most horrific war. That great conflict will culminate with the Second Coming of Jesus Christ back to the earth.

The Armageddon clock marks the countdown to Antichrist making the false peace covenant described in Daniel 9:27. The next page shows an ongoing timeline of issues and events leading to that moment.

The secular doomsday clock watchers hope that, by posting the warnings of impending nuclear war and other catastrophes, they can somehow avert reaching that midnight hour they so fear. This is what, for example, those who believe they can institute the "Great Reset" believe they, in their god-like confidence in their own ability, can accomplish.

But there is one thing and one thing only that can help humankind avoid the coming judgment and wrath of that midnight hour. That is repentance and turning to the Lord Jesus Christ, who came to die as a sacrifice for the sin into which people have been born since the Fall in Eden.

God has set the doomsday clock, and His second hand hasn't stopped moving toward that midnight moment. My own belief, along with many of His watchers on the wall of Bible prophecy, believe the clock's second hand is much closer to twelve seconds away than the ninety seconds away the authorities of the Bulletin of Atomic Scientists recently placed it.

The people of earth are on the cusp of being thrust into that midnight hour. You don't want to be one who is left behind to suffer that time of horror Jesus said will be the worst of all in human history (Mathew 24:21).

The Millstone Milestone

As regular readers of my books and commentaries perhaps know, and as I touched on earlier in this book, I'm convinced that all children below

Armageddon Clock

YEAR	MINUTES UNTIL ARMAGEDDON	SIGNIFICANT EVENT(S)
1800s	30	Although Jews have been returning to the land of promise a few at a time since their last scattering, it wasn't until the 1800s that they started going home in significant numbers. Jews were in the majority in the area by 1880. Large portions of land were purchased, bringing about more and more rural Jewish communities. As the Zionist movement gained backing, plans were made to return on a widening scale.
1914	25	The Jewish population reached 85,000 by the time World War I began in 1914. This compared to only 5,000 populating the land early in the previous century.
1917	20	British Foreign Secretary Arthur J. Balfour issued, on behalf of England, the Balfour Declaration on November 17, 1917. The Balfour declaration indicated approval of the Jewish goal of bringing about a Jewish state in Palestine.
1939	17	Adolf Hitler and the Nazis carried out persecution against all Jews within Hitler's sphere of influence. While Hitler, along with the Arab enemies of the Jews in Palestine, turned up the heat of persecution against the Jewish race, the British, the controlling authority in Palestine, developed a White Paper severely restricting Jewish immigration.
1940–1945	15	Adolf Hitler's Germany perpetrated genocide upon the Jewish race, during which more than 6 million Jews were murdered in the Holocaust.
1947	12	The Dead Sea Scrolls were found at Qumran, validating much of Old Testament writings. Jewish leadership plans a return to Zion (Jerusalem) for the purpose of establishing a nation.
1948	5	Israel was reborn as a nation on May 14, 1948. Jews are back in their promised land, just as prophesied for the last days by all Bible prophets.

the age of accountability will go to be with Christ at the Rapture of the Church. My contention isn't based on having a grandpa's heart for children, which I do. Rather, it is centered upon the Word of One who also has an all-consuming love for children. And I can prove I'm in very good company when it comes to that soft spot for little ones.

The very character of our Heavenly Father is at stake in the matter of all children below the age of accountability going to be with the Lord when He calls at the moment of Rapture. We see this magnificent character through God made manifest in the flesh, His Son, the second member of the Godhead. Consider what Jesus said:

> And said, Verily I say unto you, Except ye be converted, and become as little children, ye shall not enter into the kingdom of heaven. Whosoever therefore shall humble himself as this little child, the same is greatest in the kingdom of heaven. And whoso shall receive one such little child in my name receiveth me. But whoso shall offend one of these little ones which believe in me, it were better for him that a millstone were hanged about his neck, and that he were drowned in the depth of the sea. (Matthew 18:3–6)

Jesus' words make clear beyond question His love for those who are too young to be aware that they're born sinners and separated from God, thus need a Savior to reconcile them to their Creator. These humble "little ones" have the very spirit of innocence God requires in order to inhabit Heaven. They're in this state until they're convicted by the Holy Spirit that they need the Savior and are capable of accepting or rejecting the offer of God's grace through the salvation process.

Those who harm—"offend"—such innocent ones and keep them from coming to the Lord reserve for themselves the most severe of punishments. Jesus' "millstone" reference is an indicator of how those who prey on children, abuse them, or do anything to hinder them from learning about Jesus and His love for them are destined for the most hellish eternity imaginable.

My thoughts go to one well-known actor of past years—one of the most famous. I remember his actress daughter, also one of Hollywood's most famous, saying in an interview that when she was a child, her father mocked her for wanting to go to Sunday school with a neighbor family. He ridiculed her, saying she was a fool for believing in all that Jesus stuff.

She once said that in those days she would sit on the curb waiting for a neighboring family to stop by to pick her up for church and Sunday school. I do believe the woman is saved, but totally confused, still being a Hollywood icon with no substantial Bible education by a Christ-centered body of believers. What a punishment such a now-deceased father must be receiving, given the precious gift of a child, then to have "offended" that child in such a way.

We as a nation have now reached the point that Hollywood and all of our culture are "offending" the children of America. This, it seems, is taking place worldwide as well. As a world generation, we've reached a "millstone milestone," if you'll allow the attempt at alliteration in this section's title.

A news excerpt from several years ago makes my point:

> The boom in LGBT content for children has continued, with yet another classic getting a Pride makeover.
>
> According to Christianity Daily, the fairytale Cinderella will be coming to Amazon Prime in September with a "LGBTQ sexless godmother," played, unsurprisingly, by male homosexual Billy Porter. Porter told CBS that the new version will be "a classic fairytale for a new generation."
>
> The BBC is also plugging a new children's book called My Daddies, the story of a motherless little girl adopted by two men. This book was newsworthy not because there is any shortage of this sort of thing lately, but because it is "the first book of its kind to be written and illustrated by same-sex adoptive parents" and "the first picture book about two gay dads with both an LGBT author and illustrator."[11]

We are barraged daily with the wickedness of Sodom and Gomorrah-like evil, like what is represented by the above. This is "offending" little ones at a level probably not seen since the time of Sodom and Gomorrah.

With the murders in their mother's wombs—and even after birth—by the abortionists, and with the approval of governments, we have indeed reached a "millstone milestone."

The Tribulation will see that millstone of condemnation placed around the necks of all who have participated in such treatment of children as part of deliberately turning their backs on the God of Heaven. Perhaps this evil will be the proverbial straw that breaks the camel's back. Maybe that milestone has been reached as the stench of this world reaches the nostrils of our God.

Perhaps the midnight hour of the doomsday clock is at hand. Maybe God's intolerable level of evil and wickedness against the children—the most helpless among us—like in Lot's day in Sodom has been reached. The Rapture of the Church and the removal of such little ones out of harm's way might be very near indeed.

Discernment of the lateness of the prophetic hour is critical. Again, the Lord exhorts believers of the Church Age:

> And when you see all these things begin to come to pass, then look up, and lift up your head, for your redemption is drawing near. (Luke 21:28)

The Powers That Be

JONATHAN C. BRENTNER, a writer, blogger, and Bible teacher who is a good friend as well as a collaborator on and contributor to several of my projects, offered some keen insight in a recent article for the Harbingers Daily website. He begins with a 1961 quote from philosopher and author Aldous Huxley:

> The transhumanists of our day talk openly about eliminating the "god gene" in people. They say this will reduce the "hostility" they believe arises from "religious passion." Steiner saw this coming long ago.

Then, Brentner continues:

> More recently, philosopher and author Aldous Huxley spoke these words at the California Medical School in 1961 (please read these words carefully):
>
> > There will be, in the next generation or so, a pharmacological method of making people love their servitude, and producing dictatorship without tears, so to speak, producing a

kind of painless concentration camp for entire societies, so that people will in fact have their liberties taken away from them, but will rather enjoy it, because they will be distracted from any desire to rebel by propaganda or brainwashing, or brainwashing enhanced by pharmacological methods. And this seems to be the final revolution.

Huxley's words represent the playbook from which the globalists operate today. What he talked about in 1961 has become reality in 2023. "Pharmaceutical methods" are the weapon of choice for transhumanists seeking to change humanity by combining humans with machines.

In 2021, a video appeared on the World Economic Forum (WEF) website showing a smiling young man while the narrator said this about the future, "You will own nothing and be happy.

Does this not match the words of Huxley? People will never welcome servitude, but Huxley predicted that someday they will because of "pharmacological methods."[12]

The transhumanism assault on humankind is a major element in Lucifer's blueprint to bring into existence a New World Order. Thus, through diabolical agents such as those within the World Economic Forum, the prophesied regime of Antichrist is coming into view. God's Word addresses this evil force that's doing its worst in bringing the man of sin to power.

I often use the phrase "the powers that be." Much is tied up in that expression—more than even the most spiritually astute might suspect. Usually, in considering these "powers," we look at the Apostle Paul's heads-up in his letter to the Ephesians. Here again is what he said:

For we wrestle not against flesh and blood, but against principalities, against powers, against the rulers of the darkness of this world, against spiritual wickedness in high places. (Ephesians 6:12)

It has always been relatively easy to understand who these supernatural "powers and principalities" are. Not long ago, discernment that this warning involves human minions as well as demonic entities wasn't so easily recognized. But the progression of stage-setting for soon fulfillment has changed that.

The unfolding of prophetic progression continues at a pace that's difficult to keep up with. And—again, at the risk of being accused of being Amerocentric—I believe we can see most every element, every Satanic influence, operating within this apex nation of world history. America, the most materially blessed and one of the most spiritually blessed nations, is now host to minions of the deadliest sort. Their parasitic infestation grows more horrific by the day.

The spread of sin within the nation has reached the very thinking processes of at least half of our populace. Our leadership, particularly at the national level, exhibits the Romans 1:28, "reprobate" mindset with elected representatives of the people throwing caution to the winds of destruction. They've reached the point that the printing presses can't keep up with the amounts of money they ravenously want to spend.

They now seek to join the globalist powers that be in embracing the digital economic madness. They can, through electronic transfer, instantly create revenue for their every desire. They can control all people by controlling buying and selling. It is almost certainly the precursor to the Antichrist 666 system of Revelation 13:16–18.

Indeed, the love of money is proving to be at the root of all sorts of evil.

The powers that be, led—willingly or not—by the father of lies, himself, are spreading their reprobate mind infection to the point that evil is metastasizing uncontrollably.

Inventor of mRNA vaccines Dr. Robert Malone, having worked with the U.S. Department of Defense (DOD) for many years, warns that a war is being waged by the government for control of people's minds, and that social media platforms are being weaponized in this war and are "actively employed" by the intelligence community to influence what people think and feel.

"This new battleground, in which your mind and your thoughts, your very emotions are the battleground. It is not about territory," Malone said during a recent interview for Epoch TV's "American Thought Leaders" program. "…Members of a specific "influencer cloud" can be tracked using the military spy technology called the Gorgon Stare, said Malone. This spy technology is capable of detecting movements including what car you drive, who gets in your car, and where you go, he said.

The Gorgon Stare is a surveillance technology, originally created to target terrorist groups, that utilizes high-tech cameras mounted on drones to capture video images of large areas, such as entire cities. Then artificial intelligence is used to analyze the surveillance footage.

Arthur Holland Michel, author of the book, Eyes in the Sky: The Secret Rise of Gorgon Stare and How It Will Watch Us All, called this technology the "pinnacle of aerial surveillance" during a 2019 interview with the CATO Institute and said the things he learned while writing the book were so troubling, they kept him up at night.

The human powers are totally sold out to the one who will deliver them the authority to bring about the all-controlling, one-world regime demanded by those within the WEF. This is prophetically scheduled, of course, to bring about not utopia, but Hell on earth.

The Lord Jesus' dealing with Satan and rejecting his proposition proves Satan could offer the world's kingdoms at that moment:

And the devil took him up and showed him all the kingdoms of the world in a moment of time, and said to him, "To you I will give all this authority and their glory, for it has been delivered to me, and I give it to whom I will. If you, then, will worship me, it will all be yours." (Luke 4:5–7)

Some believe Satan no longer has that authority, because Jesus took back the title deed to the earth with His death, burial and Resurrection. The devil, they believe, can no longer offer the world to his human followers.

Well, all we see at the moment is that those powers that be are now creating that New World Order we've heard much about for so long. (In that regard, Pete Garcia's and my book, *New World Order: Worlds in Collision and the Coming Rebirth of Liberty*, deals in depth with this swiftly developing, satanic regime. I recommend reading that book to get quickly briefed on the situation.[14]) The developments toward bringing in the last seven years before Christ's Second Advent are now in place. This means the Rapture of believers is on the very brink of taking place.

Shaking Down Sodom

America's national political system has been less than virtuous from the beginning. Duels have even been fought as part of the process, with, for example, former Treasury Secretary Alexander Hamilton being killed by Vice President Aaron Burr in July of 1804. So it isn't surprising that a sin-drenched national milieu has produced Mafia-like shakedowns and extortion, blackmail, and every other nefarious political tactic.

We've seen it time after time, issue after issue. Leaders of movements wanting their way politically—usually pushing demands involving forcing American taxpayers to pay for their more often than not ungodly plans—threaten businesses and even elected authorities in order to achieve their goals.

Whereas Mafioso might urge a business to take out their "insurance" against destruction of their business or even breakage of their knees, these political shakedown artists operate similarly. They often suggest that an elected official vote and/or implement plans the shakedowners want—as protection against having the organization (often a race-based monocracy) work against the extorted elected official's political futures.

It has become the American way of local, state, and national politics. And, as I believe biblically prophetic progression has reached the end of this Church Age, I think it is probably accurate to say—as Barack Obama's one-time pastor Jeremiah Wright might say—America's chickens have come home to roost.

I use the subheading "Shaking Down Sodom" to convey yet again how our beloved nation seems to fit the Sodom of Lot's day. Jesus said that things would be like they were in the wicked times in Sodom, when God will suddenly and without remedy cast judgment upon an incorrigible, ungodly, rebellious people. This will be done, just as when the Lord first removed Lot, whom He viewed as righteous. It will be the Rapture that removes God's children and begins bringing to an end through judgment and wrath humankind's final rebellion against Heaven's intended order.

The United States fits the Luke 17:28–30 Sodom model, as I've written before. Of all nations on the planet, many in severely failing economic situations, America is still going along pretty much business as usual, just as Sodom of Lot's day. Beneath that business-as-usual flow, however, beats the heart of wickedness perhaps matched by no other nation on earth. Our technological advancement, along with unparalleled freedoms, has produced a level of evil unavailable to any other generation.

And this brings me to the point I hope to make.

Having reached this Sodom-like level, America is ripe for a radical change of monumental proportion. As a matter of fact, Satan's desired installation of his Antichrist regime, it seems to me, cannot be achieved so long as this constitutional republic as configured since its founding stands. It must be destroyed—or at least disassembled. In that regard, we have been witnessing such a restructuring on a global scale.

The Ephesians 6:12 human minions within the United Nations, the World Economic Forum, and other New World Order institutional bodies are stripping America's wealth and, even more profoundly, its structure, once moored and governed by Judeo-Christian principles. And many within our representative government at the national level are willing to allow this undoing of our nation out of motives governed by the desire for personal wealth and power.

Those who understand what's truly happening to our country recognize the collusion and subterfuge taking place within the federal government. We have observed and chronicled agencies like the FBI, CIA, and others that once protected America become totally politicized and joined to the globalists' cabal. They have made American citizens the targets for purposes of bringing the nation into compliance with all of their global plans. We've watched these forces, now turned totally to the dark side, do all within their power to bring down an America-First president. And they have, in effect, managed to do just that.

We have watched, standing by almost helplessly, elections being stolen. Again, seemingly because of a desire to achieve personal wealth and power, elected representatives of both major political parties have chosen to not rock the boat in which they float within the Washington swamp. It is indeed a "uniparty"—as charged—that we are now becoming enslaved by, as the American electoral process no longer exists as intended at our founding.

The current American president, Joseph Biden, likely compromised by conflicts of interest with China, Ukraine, and other international entities, along with the military-industrial complex warned about by President Dwight Eisenhower, has the nation bogged in commitments that drain America's wealth by trillions of dollars—which, incidentally, we no longer possess. Yet this once-great nation continues to stand, although shaken both externally and internally. Like Sodom of Lot's day, business as usual within the US even seems to hold up the collapse of much of the rest of the world.

The most stringent efforts of the Ephesians 6:12 extortionists-shakedown artists who are *the powers that be*—the powers and principalities, both human and demonic—have not yet succeeded in bringing America down so they can plunder its wealth.

And they won't succeed by their ever-increasing, wicked efforts. Like in the case of Sodom, America and the entire, wicked world system will come crashing down by the upheaval God's judgment will bring at the Rapture.

We are in the throes of end-times midnight madness, precisely the way Jesus said.

7

Valley of Derision

I FIND THE FOLLOWING WORDS some of the best as a preface to addressing God's mighty restraint on evil:

> Psalm 2 is a picture of God's great plan of redemption. It shows that no evil imagination of Satan to destroy humanity through the demonic manipulation of kings and rulers of nations will ever work. The thief has come to steal, kill and destroy people, but actually he is coming against God.
>
> Remember how Satan worked through kings to kill all the baby boys when both Moses and Jesus were in infants? I can imagine God sitting in the Heavens and laughing at that failed plan.
>
> Psalm 2:1–4 also has reference to Revelation 11:18 and Revelation 19:15. These verses refer to the culmination of God's plan of redemption and how He will take care of business in end times.[15]

The Lord tells, through the prophet Joel, the dire recompense for the rebellious evil of opposing His righteousness:

> Proclaim ye this among the Gentiles; Prepare war, wake up the mighty men, let all the men of war draw near; let them come up:

Beat your plowshares into swords, and your pruning hooks into spears: let the weak say, I am strong. Assemble yourselves, and come, all ye heathen, and gather yourselves together round about: thither cause thy mighty ones to come down, O Lord. Let the heathen be wakened, and come up to the valley of Jehoshaphat: for there will I sit to judge all the heathen round about. Put ye in the sickle, for the harvest is ripe: come, get you down; for the press is full, the fats overflow; for their wickedness is great. Multitudes, multitudes in the valley of decision: for the day of the Lord is near in the valley of decision. (Joel 9–14)

We are at this moment very near the beginning of that time, at the end of which everyone will be gathered into the Valley of Jehoshaphat—the killing field of Armageddon. As Joel declares, we now see wickedness growing daily, even hourly. It is indeed an exponential growth of evil directed primarily at God's prescribed order of things for the earth.

Armies of the world, particularly those of nations primary to prophetic fulfillment, have already turned pruning hooks and ploughshares into swords and spears that are the incredibly powerful instruments of modern warfare. They have awakened the warriors and gathered them, as witnessed by Russia's assaults on Ukraine and China's voracious glances at Taiwan. The world is, to any observer with a rational eye for developments, preparing to make war.

It's just a matter of time until the multitudes will gather to oppose God and storm toward His touchstone to humanity, Jerusalem and the Temple Mount. They will at first rage against one another, each wanting to make that Satanic prize—Jerusalem and Mount Moriah—their conquest. They will be filled with the madness their father, the devil, has planted in their reprobate minds. They will then see the black skies above earth split apart and the glory of Heaven beaming through as the Lord of lords and King of kings and His army of redeemed saints begin their descent.

Today we are in a valley of *decision*, of sorts. The decision is whether to be on the side of the heathens destined to oppose God and His righteousness, and thus be in colleague with those who will face Christ the King in the Valley of Jehoshaphat, or whether to be on God's side by accepting His only way to redemption, thus to be on the side that opposes the wickedness we see proliferating in every direction we look.

Another valley I think we can see very plainly at this time is a valley of *derision*. It is a place of profound struggle against the powers and principalities in high places of Ephesians 6:12. Christians who determine to fight the evil that opposes God's righteousness comprise the nucleus of this force. While many others who do not know Christ as their Lord also battle against wickedness, God's people are the glue that holds fast the frontline resistance to the assaults by Lucifer's minions.

Paul the apostle says it is the Restrainer who will hold back the assaults of evil and wickedness until He is taken out of the way. The Holy Spirit is that Restrainer, and He works primarily by indwelling all who know Christ for salvation. So it is the believers of this age who must continue the struggle, empowered by God the Holy Spirit. And there is plenty of evidence to validate that God is restraining in these times so near when He will call the Church out of this doomed world of rebelliousness.

We have witnessed time after time, for example, blockage of legislative efforts that would take America into dictatorship. The evil continues to advance, but is not allowed to completely infect the world with the sin that will cause God's judgment and wrath to finally fall upon the incorrigible rebels who oppose His righteousness.

The time will come when "earth dwellers" will have their way, mostly unimpeded by God's governance. But this condition won't last long. Devastating things will begin to happen as God prepares for Jesus to return and put an end to all evil, wickedness, and rebellion.

The Lord has these anti-God, anti-Christ forces in derision at this very moment. His Holy Spirit is holding back Satan's all-out assault until the Church is taken to be with Jesus in the Rapture.

Derision in Microcosm

When witnessing what's going on in the American political world over the past months, we can come to one conclusion: The Lord is at work directing all things into eschatological channels of His own design. Those who adamantly oppose godliness are mostly on the side of one political party. They are for everything the Lord in Heaven says He is against. God is making that opposition clear by confusing them for all the world to see.

This opposition party to God's desires for human conduct adheres to going against the Lord's key principles of life. They are for the murder of the unborn and even those just born; they are for abortion under the guise of giving women the right to choose. They are champions of men having sexual relations with other men and women having sexual relations with other women.

This is happening even under the auspices of the so-called clergy who approve of this unbiblical activity. They define marriage as being, basically, anything one wants it to be—a man can marry another man or a woman another woman. Even more insanely, some have been given the go-ahead by these anti-God adherents to marry their animals or even inanimate objects of their affection.

In earlier times, reports of things going on under this "progressive" mindset would have defied logic. But now, the abnormal—even abhorrent—activity is seen by these anti-God forces as not only okay, but as more mainstream than the formerly normal human activity.

I refer, for example, to the views that have been developing regarding pedophilia. Even courses at the university level now hold that including children in sexual activity with adults is to be "normed"—not considered psychological dysfunction or criminal activity, but just an alternate way of looking at things.

As we've looked at before, people are now perfectly "normal" if they consider themselves to be a gender other than what their birth certificate shows. By this, they're saying the Creator didn't know what He was doing.

He has no right to declare who is man, who is woman, or whatever else they want to be, I guess.

Grade-school children and even younger are being subjected to transvestites who try to lure them into becoming like themselves. The "progressive" mindset considers parents "haters" and evil holdouts to human advancement if they oppose having their children inculcated in such a manner.

The party of choice among these anti-God forces applauds and holds up as icons of the new wave of society a presidential candidate who kisses his "husband" on stage at political rallies. The mainstream news and entertainment media embrace this as normal and even preferable. By this, they applaud shaking off the bonds of godly restraint as put forth in God's Holy Word.

Democrat Mayor Pete Buttigieg, an avowed homosexual married to another male, has voiced the "progressive" thinking in wishing to throw off godly restraints as America moves forward in history. He once said he condemned Vice President Mike Pence's view of morality and Christianity. He declared that America must change from its narrow definition of morality by saying it's time to move on from that old mode to something more "inclusive" and "humane." By this it means he is unhappy with those who are against the lifestyle of the LGBTQ+ (and P for pedophile) community because of narrow-minded beliefs in biblical precepts for godly living.

The message is that he is in favor of throwing off all these moralistic bands that inhibit people from doing what is right in their own eyes. Mr. Buttigieg is just one of many within today's Democratic party who expresses opposition to God's way of conducting life. Remember the vitriolic comments by one of the campaign planners for presidential candidate Bernie Sanders. He declared, in a video secretly obtained by the Veritas organization, that if Sanders and associates are elected, he will immediately and summarily kill some who oppose them. He will then make sure, he said, that others are sent to retraining camps to get their minds right. Still others would be locked away in labor-camp gulags, never again to interfere with progressive movement.

Make no mistake, the evil that inspired the Nazi thugs of Hitler's time continues to interact with the would-be diabolists of these troubled days. If given the chance, they would do exactly what this campaign associate of one of the former leading Democratic candidates promised. This is not to say all who are in that political party are of the same mindset as this campaign worker. But, neither were many in 1930s Germany of the same mindset as the Nazis and the Führer.

The mentality just described as growing in our time is a reminder of just where this generation stands on God's prophetic timeline. The Lord had something to say about the ultimate outcome of such rebellion as outlined in Psalms chapter 2.

His Word begins in that prophetic condemnation passage with a question, then gives a devastating answer to all who would throw off the moral restraints He has prescribed. The one who will judge this rebellious world is none other than the person God declares to be His Son in this prophecy. We have watched God hold the opposition political party in almost complete derision at times. It is but a taste of things to come when, at the end of this age, the Lord Jesus Christ will judge all whom He calls "earth dwellers"—those who are in rebellion against Him.

Again, here is what the Lord says about what is going on now and into eternity:

Why do the heathen rage, and the people imagine a vain thing? The kings of the earth set themselves, and the rulers take counsel together, against the Lord, and against his anointed, saying, Let us break their bands asunder, and cast away their cords from us. He that sitteth in the heavens shall laugh: the Lord shall have them in derision. Then shall he speak unto them in his wrath, and vex them in his sore displeasure. Yet have I set my king upon my holy hill of Zion. I will declare the decree: the Lord hath said unto me, Thou art my Son; this day have I begotten thee. Ask of me, and

I shall give thee the heathen for thine inheritance, and the uttermost parts of the earth for thy possession. Thou shalt break them with a rod of iron; thou shalt dash them in pieces like a potter's vessel. Be wise now therefore, O ye kings: be instructed, ye judges of the earth. Serve the Lord with fear, and rejoice with trembling. Kiss the Son, lest he be angry, and ye perish from the way, when his wrath is kindled but a little. Blessed are all they that put their trust in him. (Psalms 2:1–12)

8

Restraining the Madness

THE MADNESS THAT HAS INFECTED all societies and cultures in these closing days of the Church Age (Age of Grace) seems to have no limits. We are in the time of Romans 1:28 and the reprobate mindset all who reject God will suffer. But God's Word has promised that the Holy Spirit will hold back the anti-Godliness until the very time God's people, the Church, are removed.

And the Church must be taken from this fallen sphere before Antichrist, the son of perdition, can come to power.

> The phrase "reprobate mind" is found in Romans 1:28 in reference to those whom God has rejected as godless and wicked. They "suppress the truth by their wickedness," and it is upon these people that the wrath of God rests (Romans 1:18).
>
> The Greek word translated "reprobate" in the New Testament is *adokimos*, which means literally "unapproved, that is, rejected; by implication, worthless (literally or morally)."
>
> Paul describes two men named Jannes and Jambres as those who "resist the truth: men of corrupt minds, reprobate concerning the faith" (2 Timothy 3:8).

Here the reprobation is regarding the resistance to the truth because of corrupt minds. In Titus, Paul also refers to those whose works are reprobate:

They profess that they know God; but in works they deny him, being abominable, and disobedient, and unto every good work reprobate. (Titus 1:16).

Therefore, the reprobate mind is one that is corrupt and worthless.

As we can see in the verses above, people who are classified as having a reprobate mind have some knowledge of God and perhaps know of His commandments.

However, they live impure lives and have very little desire to please God. Those who have reprobate minds live corrupt and selfish lives. Sin is justified and acceptable to them. The reprobates are those whom God has rejected and has left to their own devices.[16]

Seeing all the wickedness proliferating exponentially and knowing the subterranean evil that is unseen, we might throw up our hands and ask a legitimate question: "What hope is there?" It looks forever more like Satan has already reached his goals of turning everything upside down, of thwarting all efforts to stand in his wicked, lawless way.

We've gone over all of the cultural and societal rot—all the perversion that has seemingly permeated every aspect of life. Even children are now, for example, targets of the devilish schemers who have public school officials and many courts agreeing that parents can't intervene with their kids being inculcated or even transgendered. This seems to be perhaps the last or most satanically insane accomplishment taking place as this generation approaches the Tribulation era.

Yet there is doubtless much more to come, and there seems to be no opposition to what we fear will eventuate. The avalanche of absolute evil, it appears, will arrive sooner rather than later.

The world is building toward war—war that, it is almost certain, if it comes to full fruition, will result in nuclear annihilation for most, if not all, of the planet's population.

Thanks be to the Creator of all that is. This world is on a controlled demolition schedule—like one of those huge, ancient hotels that must be brought down so something new and beautiful can be constructed in its place. This is exactly what is happening, in prophetic terms.

The world and all we see happening, as my friend Jan Markell—one of the most listened-to program hosts in Christian radio—has stated, isn't the world falling apart. It is all falling into place. Perhaps that was a paraphrase of Jan's comment, but you get the gist. The Lord is in charge of this demolition—or at least He is in complete control of how He long ago foretold how things would come together so a new, beautiful, Heaven-directed earth construction can occur.

An appropriate question to ask in light of all this is whether God the Holy Spirit, the third Person of the Trinity, is acting as an unseen agent in controlling the demolition of the world's infrastructures. Is He keeping everything from crumbling to complete rubble through His supernatural engineering? That is, is God still acting as Restrainer, as promised?

For the mystery of iniquity doth already work: only he [the Restrainer or Holy Spirit] who now letteth [Restrains evil] will let [Restrain evil], until he be taken out of the way. And then shall that Wicked be revealed, whom the Lord shall consume with the spirit of his mouth, and shall destroy with the brightness of his coming. (2 Thessalonians 2:7–8)

I believe this means the Holy Spirit will hold back evil until He withdraws from that role. This will happen when the Rapture occurs. At that electrifying, "twinkling-of-an-eye" moment, those whom He indwells, Christ will call believers of this age into Heaven. Then the demolition of the earth and its evil, humanistic, systems will totally crash to rubble. God's wrath and judgment will fall like it did on Sodom and Gomorrah.

Those who believe and expound upon the Rapture of the Church are met at best with severe criticism and at worst with accusation of being escapists who are leading people to not recognize Antichrist when that beast appears. These critics—and there are many within even evangelical Christian circles—lack understanding of God's great purposes for the Rapture.

My late friend Jack Kinsella, who wrote daily for his great ministry blog, *The Omega Letter,* had an explanation for those misguided believers. Here's what he wrote, in part:

> The purpose of the seven-year Tribulation Period is two-fold. The first reason is to fulfill Daniel's prophecy of the 70 Weeks. The angel told Daniel that:
>
> > "Seventy weeks are determined upon thy people and upon thy holy city, to finish the transgression, and to make an end of sins, and to make reconciliation for iniquity, and to bring in everlasting righteousness, and to seal up the vision and prophecy, and to anoint the most Holy." (Daniel 9:24)
>
> Note there are six elements to the fulfillment of this prophecy. First, to finish Israel's sin—the rejection of the Messiah at the First Advent.
>
> Then there is a skip forward in time to His Second Advent, at which time an end will be made of sin; reconciliation will be made for Israel's iniquity; everlasting righteousness will be introduced to Israel; Israel's Scriptures will be vindicated by the fulfillment of all prophecy; and finally, the return of Christ at the conclusion of the war of Armageddon, at which time He will be anointed and will take His seat at the Throne of David.
>
> Between the First and Second Advents, there is the Church Age, a "mystery" unrevealed to the Hebrew prophets. That is why Daniel's outline of 490 years of Israeli history doesn't anticipate

a gap between the "cutting off of the Messiah" at the end of the sixty-nine weeks of years and the confirmation of the covenant by the antichrist at the onset of the 70th (Daniel 9:27).

From Daniel's perspective, it is an unbroken narrative of what would befall "his people" (the Jews) and "his holy city" (Jerusalem), culminating with the "anointing of the Most Holy" at the conclusion of the 70th week and the ushering in of Isaiah's Millennial Kingdom. There is no role set aside for the Church in prophecy during the 70th Week since it is reserved for Israel's national redemption and their acceptance of the Messiah.

The Church has, by definition, already accepted the Messiah and was redeemed at the Cross.

The second purpose Scripture gives for the Tribulation Period is that it is a period of judgment against those who reject Christ and embrace the antichrist.

Since Christians who accept Christ were already judged at the Cross, there is no role set aside for the Church in the judgments pronounced because, "Neither repented they of their murders, nor of their sorceries, nor of their fornication, nor of their thefts" (Revelation 9:21).

- Repentance is a necessary condition of salvation. It is that repentance that causes us to seek forgiveness at the Cross in the first place. Since believers in the Church Age became believers by repenting, there is no purpose for bringing the judgment of an unrepentant world on the Church.

- [To clarify, Jack said in another article: "The gifts and calling of God are without repentance. He isn't going to change His mind. You need to change yours." The definition of repentance is a change of mind that results in a change of action.]

The Rapture isn't a "Great Escape," contrary to popular belief. The Rapture occurs when the restraining influence of the Holy Spirit is removed with the Church to allow the onset of the 7-year period of unrestrained evil that occurs during the Tribulation (2nd Thessalonians 2:7).

The Rapture is the Blessed Hope of the Church, but its primary purpose is not so much a "rescue mission" as it is a necessary function of the withdrawal of the Holy Spirit's ministry of restraining evil. Since we are indwelt by the Holy Spirit, when the Restrainer is withdrawn, so are we since we are His vessels.

Therefore, it is certain to conclude that the Church won't be here for the Tribulation itself since withdrawing the indwelling of the Holy Spirit from the believing Church would leave them spiritually defenseless at a time of maximum need, something Jesus promised He would never do.[17]

So fear not, believers. God is in full control of the demolition we are witnessing. He is indeed acting as an undercover operative in this cesspool of evil the globalists elite—those powers and principalities of Ephesians 6:12—are perpetrating. How can we be sure? By understanding that the Lord neither slumbers nor sleeps. This is observable by examining how He has kept the matter of the Iranian nuclear weapons development under complete control.

Bible prophecy predicts the mountainous area currently being used to work on Iran's nuclear designs will be destroyed. In the Elam prophecy, it is foretold that it will become uninhabitable. This portends a nuclear strike or nuclear radiation escaping as a result of an attack.

This hasn't happened despite great tensions we've all seen in the news. President Trump put in place many options to hold back Iran's deadly intentions to produce weapons that would eliminate the hated Jewish state. President Biden has, tacitly, given the ayatollahs permission to resume their development—which they say are for peaceful uses only.

This is an attempted deception that even Mr. Biden's administration State Department people certainly know is a lie.

This, of course, is to the great consternation of Israeli Prime Minister Benjamin Netanyahu and his Israel Defense Forces (IDF) generals. The following excerpt frames this angst:

> Israeli Prime Minister Benjamin Netanyahu has vowed that Israel will never allow Iran to develop "nuclear capability to carry out its genocidal goal of eliminating Israel" during a joint press conference with visiting U.S. Secretary of Defense Lloyd Austin in Jerusalem on Monday.
>
> "My policy as prime minister of Israel is clear. I will never allow Iran the nuclear capability to carry out its genocidal goal of eliminating Israel.
>
> "And Israel will continue to defend itself against Iran's aggression and terrorism," said Netanyahu.[18]

The prime minister has stated on many occasions that the IDF will use all means necessary to keep Iran from having a nuclear weapon. Nuclear action would seem necessary, if the laboratories within the Bushehr Mountains are to be destroyed. But I believe the Holy Spirit, as a covert operative, has given Israel the means to at least delay the more devastating and possibly prophesied nuclear strike option. The Restrainer is at work!

> Iranian media reported an electrical problem at the Natanz, the country's main uranium enrichment facility....
>
> "The incident caused no casualties or contamination," Iran's Atomic Energy Organization spokesman Behrouz Kamalvandi said, adding that "electricity was affected at the Natanz facility."
>
> The incident comes one day after President Hassan Rouhani inaugurated a chain of 164 advanced 164 IR-6 uranium

enrichment centrifuges at the site in a televised event commemo-rating Iran's National Day of Nuclear Technology.[19]

Experts have determined that it was without doubt a cyber attack by Israeli covert forces. So Iran's design on eliminating Israel is again thwarted—at least delayed. This is God's staying hand at work!

Be assured: God remains busy behind the scenes. Despite election cheating and all the other evil that look to be winning in Satan's end-times quest, the Restrainer will continue to restrain until Christ calls His own to be with Him.

Reset vs. Restrainer

There should be no question now in the spiritually attuned minds of Bible prophecy students. The principalities and powers in high places of Ephesians 6:12 are in full throttle. They intend to use the 2020 presidential election theft to galvanize their one-world, tower-building effort.

Global warming didn't do it. Following that lie, the climate-change ruse hasn't done it. Now, with more than six years of inflicting every sort of prevarication and *coup d'état* attempt by the globalist wickedness, they are all in for changing the earth into their own utopian concept. At the heart of that blueprint is the term we've heard over and over since the 2020 presidential campaign in the US began: the Great Reset.

The Great Reset is thrusting ahead, seemingly unstoppable while it threatens to pierce the fabric of culture and society the founding fathers wove together so carefully back in 1776. They have corrupted this God-blessed republic through fraud and deceit that is itself prophetic in nature (read Jesus' first prophetic words as recorded in Matthew chapter 24). They have, with Lucifer-inspired cleverness, possibly put the political party and the presidential placeholder into office that will, when the blueprint is come to fruition, dissolve American sovereignty, tear down borders, and bring this nation's great assets into the globalist coffers, just as their goal has been for decades.

I use the word "possibly" because, as of this writing, there remains room for the God who brought into existence this republic time to perform yet another miracle—one like He performed in the 2016 presidential election.

Certainly, it will take a miracle directly from Heaven. Prospects for a return to sane government are not good, from the way things are shaped at this time, with the ability of those who control media and other anti-America as founded diabolists to manipulate electoral results the way they want them.

Thoughts of the Great Reset has all of the pundits on that side positively giddy. And that consists of the vast majority of those who make up America's political, news media, and business elite who anticipate their far-left candidate—whomever that will be—taking the oath of office on January of 2025.

While the following is lengthier than the excerpts I prefer to include in my books, this portion of a superb article on the matter of the Great Reset is something that will explain what the nation faces:

> [A WEF video stated that] the brainchild of the World Economic Forum [WEF,] a globalist group of powerful Deep State elites that meets every year in the Swiss ski-resort town of Davos, is the "Great Reset" aims to fundamentally reengineer industries, societies, education, agriculture, relationships, and even human beings. Its advocates are openly saying as much, with WEF boss Klaus Schwab declaring that "all aspects of our societies and economies" need to be "revamped" Even "our thinking and behavior" will have to dramatically shift, he said. A WEF statement marketing the controversial scheme also calls for a "new social contract" centered on "social justice."
>
> "Every country, from the United States to China, must participate, and every industry, from oil and gas to tech, must be

transformed," added Schwab, calling for even "stronger and more effective" government, without explaining what might happen to those that refuse. "We must build entirely new foundations for our economic and social systems." And there is no other choice but to submit, he and others declared.

In his book on COVID and the Great Reset, Schwab also vowed that life would "never" return to "normal." "The world as we knew it in the early months of 2020 is no more, dissolved in the context of the pandemic," he said, adding that the looming changes are so huge that some are now speaking of "before coronavirus" (BC) and "after coronavirus" (AC) eras.

The changes will be systemic. "The COVID19 crisis has shown us that our old systems are not fit anymore for the 21st century," Schwab declared in his speech unveiling the Great Reset in June. Beyond just social systems, Schwab also called a change in "mindsets" the "most important" issue. "We have to...bring our thinking and behavior once more into harmony with nature," he said. Read that again: Even your thinking and behavior is in the global elites' crosshairs.

"Now is the historical moment—the time—not only to fight the virus, but to shape the system for the post-corona era," he added.[20]

To understand the dangers of this plan, we only have to consider that the Chinese communist government is wholeheartedly signed on to the WEF plans to establish this Great Reset. Chinese dictator Xi Jinping is one of the most-applauded leaders when the WEF meets. This points to the almost certainty that the coronavirus (often called the "Chinese virus") has been instrumental in galvanizing the efforts to bring America down and establish the globalist elites' utopian dream.

The Great Reset—no matter the planning by those who believe they are superior not just to everyone else on earth, but to God, Himself—can't proceed without that very God's permission. They, like their father, Lucifer, have determined to put their throne above the one of the Almighty. Their neo-Tower of Babel won't be completed as long as the Restrainer is on this fallen planet. The Holy Spirit, who resides within each believer, will hold back their devilish plans until He removes all believers to Heaven.

Restrainer's Resounding Resistance

Despite that it's long past, the election of 2020 isn't over. There is, I sense, much yet to be discovered, uncovered, and, perhaps recovered, before the final period—perhaps I should say "exclamation point"—marks its finality.

At the center of that corrupt, end-of-the-age demarcation—that evil-saturated presidential election—stands Heaven's most powerful force. This holy entity of might is unseen, but it's not without resounding energy and impact. The power within its long-ago prophesied influence for this critical hour is on the very brink of revealing God to a wicked, wicked world.

We've witnessed earth's powers and principalities in government, military bastions, and media enclaves as they have coalesced to form, perhaps, the most powerful anti-God movement in history. At the same time, Heaven's force has quietly swatted away every attempt to bring in Satan's Antichrist regime. The evil has been, as I've said, almost tangible throughout every news cycle over the past six or seven years. The defense against the evil hasn't been overtly manifest, for the most part.

All of this end-of-the-age spiritual warfare, straight out of Ephesians 6:12, has seemed to be fought particularly in America. The moment Donald J. Trump became his political party's nominee, the battle roared to life in ways not seen before in my lifetime. The satanic minions were knocked off balance, losing equilibrium—and all sanity—from that moment. They are scrambling more frantically than ever to regain lost time in the globalist onslaught they began following World War II with the establishment of the United Nations.

Still, as the battle rages, the force that resists is largely hidden, spiritually speaking. But it is there, and it is a pent-up force that I sense is about to be unleashed in ways we can't fully fathom.

To many believers, it seems that God is silent, while the minions of the powers-and-principalities coalition apparently have gotten away with fraud of the first order. Mainstream media dominated by the "prince of the power of the air" proclaim at every opportunity that the election was the people speaking, and that their wishes were a change from America as founded. At least, that was the implied undercurrent flowing beneath the mainstream declaration.

Ultimately, however, it isn't even those behind the lying tongues and word processors who have that power to shape. They are but players on the stage of history—as are we all. It is the God of Heaven who determines who will be president. He raises up kings and those in authority, and He removes them, the Scripture tells us. His, alone, is the true power that determines the future (see Romans 13:1–2).

All this, and at the same time He allows free will. It is a concept beyond the finite mind's ability to comprehend. In other words, we cannot understand how He allows free will, yet at the same time controls everything absolutely. This is all wrapped up, of course, in His omnipotence—His all-powerful, hands-on governance of His created universe.

It's part of His omniscience, too—His all-consuming knowledge from eternity past into eternity future. Nothing takes Him by surprise, and there is nothing He doesn't ultimately control.

So while it might seem that resistance to evil is on the decline and the minions of evil are charging to victory in this election and in every other facet of life, the opposite is true. Again, as my friend, Jan Markell, says: "Things aren't falling apart; they are falling together"—i.e., things laid out in God's plan are coming to fruition exactly as the He says, and at a blistering pace.

The very fact that all of the cheating and fraud of the presidential election of 2020 haven't yet secured victory for those perpetrators means God and His restraining hand is still at work as powerfully as ever. That power is fueled in a mighty way by the prayers of His saints, indwelt by God the Holy Spirit.

So, whatever the outcome of that stolen election, God's will is being done, and His victory—thus ours—is absolutely assured.

> Nay, in all these things we are more than conquerors through him that loved us. (Romans 8:37)

In the supernatural battle of Reset vs. Restrainer, the winning strategy is firmly held only in the mind of God. This should give everyone who names the name of Jesus Christ great comfort. I know it does me.

Section III

Sodom and Gomorrah

Godlessness

Section III

9

Cultural and Societal Insanity

LOU DOBBS, a long-time broadcast pundit on issues and events of the day, and his guest, Eric Metaxas, were discussing the guest's new book, *Is Atheism Dead?* The conversation turned to the way culture in America has become victim of insane thinking wrapped in the term "woke."

Dobbs offered, optimistically, that he had seen his own church and pastor beginning to awaken. The congregation was awakening to the evil of things going on that were, through the insanity of woke wickedness infecting American culture and society with a deadly virus spawned by neo-Marxists, determined to change the nation into a Soviet or Maoist-style tyrannical state. He said we are awakening to what is happening. The attempted Marxist cultural revolution is being made manifest for Americans to see. There is, he believes, still a considerable majority of patriots to prevail against the globalist efforts to bring America down. The founding fathers, he said, knew that we the people need God, thus built into the founding documents that reality and provided ways to deal with such assaults. God has His hand on the nation, but we must exercise our courage to keep the nation as founded, was his exhortation.

Dobbs and his guest discussed the upside-down thinking of the leftist radicals at the forefront of the woke insanity: how it all got started with the takeover of the public educational system, with Marxism becoming ensconced in the institutions of learning, and the ideological contamination then spreading from kindergarten through twelfth grade.

Study of the real disciplines—reading, writing, arithmetic, biology, etc.—under wokeism has been cast to the back of the line of educational prerequisites. Now it has come to be that critical race theory (CRT), LGTBQ+, and other inculcation grips children of ages as young as kindergarten.

Parents are attacked by the governing elements at every stratum, from the federal level to the local school boards, for daring to assert that they, the parents, should influence curriculum. Concerned parents have been labeled "domestic terrorists" for showing up at school board meetings, demanding that their children not be taught CRT or not be subjected to boys and girls sharing the same restrooms or locker rooms at the same time.

We've all been aware of these news stories. And unless we've tuned to mostly secondary sources, not mainstream outlets, we've been bombarded by news slanted so that we're made to seem like the lunatics for disagreeing with the woke culture, and the perpetrators of the woke culture are made out to be the enlightened, sane ones in today's America.

Lou Dobbs and his guest had to admit that with the ubiquitous mainstream news and the governments in the hands of mostly woke types, it would indeed be a fight to awaken the numbers of Americans necessary to overthrow this evil. However, such a revolution of change back to sanity was possible with the awakening taking place because of the woke evil in our faces constantly.

One news item seems to somewhat support the contention:

A majority of Americans say that male and female are the only two genders, and that schools shouldn't be allowed to counsel children about gender or sexuality without parents' consent, according to the results of a survey released Monday.

The survey was conducted by Rasmussen Reports among 1,000 American adults from Dec. 21 to 22, with a margin of error of plus or minus 3 percentage points at and 95 percent confidence level. It comes amid a social media firestorm sparked by Harry Potter author J. K. Rowling, who was accused of engaging in "hate speech" for insisting that there are only two biologically distinct genders.

"Transgender activists have accused J. K. Rowling of 'hate speech' for saying it, but most Americans agree with the Harry Potter author that there are only two genders," the report said.[21]

Despite the encouraging survey result mentioned here, I must say I can't match Mr. Dobbs' optimism. I believe these years find this generation too far into the reprobate mindset of Romans 1:28. Rather than seeing a great move within our churches and among our pastors to begin rectifying the cultural rot by turning to God in all the Heaven-prescribed ways, the Church as a whole looks the other way to different priorities.

The evil and wickedness manifest through this thing called "woke" run rampant. God, through Isaiah the prophet, put it this way:

Woe unto them that call evil good, and good evil; that put darkness for light, and light for darkness; that put bitter for sweet, and sweet for bitter! Woe unto them that are wise in their own eyes, and prudent in their own sight! (Isaiah 5:20–21)

This condition of seemingly incorrigible corruption as we face the upcoming days seems to match Jesus' words about His sudden intervention into the affairs of humankind, when things will be like they were in the days of Noah and the days of Lot.

It is incumbent upon each Christian who reads this to seriously consider whether we are woke or awake. There might not be a Great Awakening taking place, as secular pundits such as Mr. Dobbs and others apparently believe. As a matter of fact, I'm convinced no such movement is coming. But it is time for each Christian to awaken to the fact that Christ's Second Advent is blazing across the prophetic horizon. First, there must come a time of horror like the world has never seen or will ever see—according to Jesus, Himself. That is the reality facing all of humanity–with the exception of those in God's family.

It is time to be awake to how near Christ's call is to His own in the air above this judgment-bound planet. This individual awakening should inspire each of us to do "our utmost for His highest," as early twentieth-century Scottish evangelist Oswald Chambers put it.

What a glorious eternal day it will be to hear our Lord and Savior say, "Well done, good, faithful, servant!"

Providential Power, Not Politics

Radio talk show host Dan Bongino was telling his audience that the evil taking place has changed America; it has dramatically diminished the nation's greatness. He concluded that those who are patriotic must resolve to fight with all their political might to counter the wickedness.

Bongino said, in effect, that it isn't any longer just disagreement within various governing or even constitutional issues that's the problem—although things concerning how to properly govern in a constitutional republic are critical. Those are important and must be vigorously defended against progressive attempts to bring down our orderly and lawfully governed way of life.

He then played a clip of two women conversing on, I presume, a progressive podcast or broadcast program. Bongino said this is the kind of evil we as a nation are up against.

The women, obviously ultra-progressive, were talking about how the transsexual agenda is all-important and must win out over influences such as Christians and their challenges to true progress in the area of transsexuality and children.

The argument one of the women made was that those who oppose the sexual/gender changes taking place in regard to the trans movement say boys have male anatomy and girls have female anatomy, and that's the way it is. They can't change that as part of being born humans. The woman then said, "Why not? Why can't people who sense, or know they are other than what they were born with, change if they want to change?"

In effect, she said it is each person's right to choose which sex they want to be, and no one should be allowed to restrict that right.

This was a serious-sounding discussion—grown women, very well spoken—declaring that individual human beings should choose their gender as their realization of which sex they are comes forth. They were talking about children as young as kindergartners making that decision.

Bongino then said, after playing the clip, this sort of thing is what will destroy this nation; it is pure wickedness—evil—setting up to totally turn America into something other than what it has been.

He said we have to fight this evil now. It's gone far beyond what formerly were merely issues of political importance. It is up to us—true patriots—to concentrate on dealing with—fighting with all we have—this demonic insanity.

Of course, he is absolutely correct. It is insanity. It is the reprobate mindset of Romans 1:28. Things are not "normal." Things we see now—every hour of every day—are more and more evil being unleashed through end-times portals into society and culture.

However, Bongino is dead wrong about how to fight it. The only armor with which to oppose this wickedness is to turn to the Lord Jesus Christ for heavenly assistance. This is why I no longer look to the political process to correct the nation's course—to "make America great." Do I mean I don't vote any longer or do what I can to work within society to fight evil legislation and even illegal, anti-American activity? No. Of course not. But now I view all political action as all but totally useless in changing things for the better. The best such action can yield is helping delay the inevitable. The world and our beloved nation are *nearing midnight*. All is headed for God's judgment and His holy wrath.

This course of devolving into prophetic oblivion is inalterable from the standpoint of our politicians and their schemes being ineffective at best and destructive at worse. Now, with the very end of the age directly in front of us on the horizon, it is time—individually, as God's royal ambassadors—to put on that machinery of waging holy war.

And, lest we be accused of calling for physical, kinetic, violent warfare, I'm referring again to the weaponry issued by the armory of Heaven to each and every believer. It's weaponry to fight a spiritual battle against the wickedness like we find within the conversation of the "progressive" women mentioned above.

But what can mere spiritual armor do to prevail against the mounting evil? God sometimes seems so distant as we face these literal circumstances. It is certain that the more the wicked one and his force ramp up the assaults, the more the Lord will provide his Church with the arsenal to oppose Satan and his minions.

Jesus said the gates of Hell, the forces of evil, will not prevail against the Church. We are God's force, indwelt by God the Holy Spirit. We will be used by the Lord of hosts to restrain this onset of evil until we are suddenly removed from the battlefield.

Here again is the arsenal each of us have been issued for battle until that marvelous moment of Rapture:

> Wherefore take unto you the whole armour of God, that ye may
> be able to withstand in the evil day, and having done all, to stand.
> Stand therefore, having your loins girt about with truth, and hav-
> ing on the breastplate of righteousness; And your feet shod with
> the preparation of the gospel of peace; Above all, taking the shield
> of faith, wherewith ye shall be able to quench all the fiery darts of
> the wicked. And take the helmet of salvation, and the sword of the
> Spirit, which is the word of God: Praying always with all prayer
> and supplication in the Spirit, and watching thereunto with all
> perseverance and supplication for all saints. (Ephesians 6:13–18)

Perdition's Propagandists Prep School

It has been taking place for decades, even longer. The American and world public have become anesthetized, or at the very least numbed, to the effects. At least half of this nation's population seems to be in a near-comatose state concerning what is right and wrong in terms of what the founding fathers meant in establishing a constitutional republic.

I refer to the incessant propagandizing of the people by a news conglomerate that mimics in most every way the Big Brother news leviathan of George Orwell's novel *1984*. The author invented the term "double-speak," defined as language that deliberately disguises, distorts, or reverses meaning to further an agenda, often by governments, corporations, marketers, or other power structures.

The novel tells of a socially stratified, post-nuclear war world ruled by three superstates—Oceania, Eastasia, and Eurasia. The ruling elite keep the "trolls" under their oppressive governmental thumb. These are the worker bees who are given just enough entertainment and mind-altering substances to imbibe to keep their noses to the grindstone of serving the state and to keep their minds off the machinations of those who govern them.

We have, since the late 1950s and even before that, been victims of the emergence of Orwell's 1949 vision of a dystopian, news-propaganda monster. It appears that perhaps two-thirds of the American populace has fallen into Orwell's "troll" category within today's political process.

Perhaps this figure is a bit of an exaggeration, but the astonishing disconnect is troubling. According to reactions I see in the matter of people understanding whether information they get is reality or propaganda, no other conclusion can be reached. Millions are falling for the lies that say they should be allowed to do what is right in their own eyes. Anyone who holds up biblical or even constitutional founding principles as the way we should behave is met with angry protestation.

Those of us who believe abortion, homosexuality, use of illicit drugs, pornography, fornication, adultery, and other such evils are wrong are seen by a vast section of the nation's population as the evil side of American society and culture.

We've witnessed the Orwellian-like news organizations of our day in action. These join that vast number in pigeonholing Christians and "moralists," as they would have it, into a corner they call "hate-mongering."

A campaign planner of one political party's candidates recently called all who oppose the leftist agenda "Nazis." He then proceeded to, in Hitler-Aryan fashion, tell those around him what he will do to the opposition once his party won. He said he would kill some and put others in gulag. The rest would go into reeducation camps to get their minds right. The mainstream, Orwellian news media, so far as I can determine, said nothing to condemn this rhetoric.

Evil doesn't change. The rhetoric, under the right conditions, will become murderous implementation when opportunity arises. There are still those with Satanic-controlled minds who would perpetrate on Americans the same sort of atrocities the Nazi beasts inflicted upon the Jews and other victims of those days.

God's Word says a time is coming when people will fall totally for the doublespeak and newspeak of those horrendous times. The ultimate Big Brother will forge a regime so powerful and evil in influence that no one, in human terms, can resist. He will have the consummate propaganda machine to brainwash and reinforce his dictatorship's absolute control. His minions are now being prepared to carry out his inculcation of the "trolls" of that Tribulation time. They will be all who are left behind because of their unbelief when Christ calls believers in the Rapture.

Today's mainstream news organizations are acting as a prep school for inflicting the future lies of the son of perdition. So it is not too far-fetched to see a bit into the future and apply prophetic Scripture, based upon what we see developing now. The nation and world are being prepared for the ultimate manifestation of the Orwellian world the author forecast with the release of his novel *1984*.

Let no man deceive you by any means: for that day shall not come, except there come a falling away first, and that man of sin be revealed, the son of perdition.... Even him, whose coming is after the working of Satan with all power and signs and lying wonders, and with all deceivableness of unrighteousness in them that perish; because they received not the love of the truth, that they might be saved. And for this cause God shall send them strong delusion, that they should believe a lie: That they all might be damned who believed not the truth, but had pleasure in unrighteousness. (2 Thessalonians 2:3, 9–12)

You don't have to be among the "trolls." Accept Christ right this moment. You will go instantaneously to be with Jesus Christ in an *atomos* of time—faster than the eye can blink—when He says, "Come up here!" (Revelation 4:2).

10

Building Back Babel

THERE IS MUCH SPECULATION, supposition, and outright pontification on the matter of America being the Babylon of Revelation chapter 18. The theological seminary types whom I consider excellent scholars in correctly analyzing Bible prophecy, in most every case, come down on the side of the Babylon in Revelation 18 to be a literal, rebuilt city that ancient one it once stood.

America, they might add, is a city-state type that fits within the Babylon system of rebellion that has plagued the world throughout human history. But the US is not the "Mystery Babylon" that will be destroyed in one hour at some point during the seven-year Tribulation.

I'm quite wishy-washy on this, because I don't see where God's Word absolutely states it will be rebuilt in its original location. It is, after all, called "Mystery Babylon." This makes it somewhat of an open question, so far as it being a literal Babylon, rebuilt in the literal former location.

That said, I will state that things presented in God's Word make it look like it most likely will be a city rebuilt in its geographical location on the plains of Shinar. I just can't visualize it being reconstructed quickly enough—that is, being completed as a great city-state and then becoming such a grandiose, powerful influence on all of the world's commerce. I can't imagine this all taking place based upon the swiftness of prophetic progression at this moment.

Babylon's ancient geographical location is almost nothing but desert. I've heard of no sign that implies significant construction of any sort is underway. Saddam Hussein had a small project or two started there to reconstruct Babylon for a tourist attraction. But that, as I understand, is in great disrepair and never amounted to much in the first place. So if the Babylon of Revelation 18 is to be the one of prophecy that will be destroyed in an hour or two—if the beginning of the Tribulation is to be sooner rather than later—somebody better get to building, and quickly.

And, even if it is constructed almost overnight, as my good friend Dr. Mark Hitchcock has suggested in his book, *The Second Coming of Babylon*, I, again, can't visualize that city-state becoming the massive boon to all the world's commerce within a short time.

Of course, there is always great leeway for miraculous activity, particularly as time is compressed during these last-days developments. This could happen. I'm just too dense in my imagination to see it coming to pass in fewer than several decades, at a minimum.

Meantime, we look at the many Babylonian-like evils taking place in America and around the globe. The anti-God wickedness we see on the rise in every direction is appalling. The Lord's patience is tremendous beyond all understanding, but it is not infinite. That is, other generations have been judged—completely wiped out—with less evil and wickedness than this rebellious world displays hourly.

America, in particular, exhibits ancient Babylonian-level blasphemy and bloodthirsty activity beyond that of the ancients. We have put into our law the right, even the demand, that nearly seventy million babies be murdered in their mother's wombs. This sort of wickedness, alone, was a major cause of God bringing down ancient Babylon and other empires. We, as a culture and society, haven't yet placed infants in the red-hot hands of an idol like Moloch, but we have allowed the unborn—and even those just born—to be sacrificed upon the altars of sexual convenience that amounts to worship of debauchery.

Satanic ritual, although disguised as art and/or entertainment, such as displayed during this year's and previous Super Bowl halftimes, points to the Babylonian nature accepted by perhaps half of the American populace.

Many worship at the altar of commerce, exhibiting a materialistic bent that doubtless would have put ancient Babylonians to shame. This unprecedented worship of the riches of this world is made possible by the technologies that have been created—those not available to those past civilizations.

One such technological platform is, of course, Amazon. We had a neighbor who ordered things from Amazon and other sources, and boxes accumulated around the front and sides of her home. Some became concerned she was deceased or ill, but that wasn't the case. She just ordered and ordered "stuff," and never even took it into the house. The many, many packages stayed out in the rain and through all other sorts of weather.

Now this smacks of a dementia, I'll admit, but the sort of culture that promotes worship of material possessions likely exacerbates the proclivity to develop forms of dementia. It is not surprising, therefore, that the following construction is in the offing.

Amazon has just unveiled the plans for its new corporate headquarters that will stand in Arlington, Virginia, directly across the Potomac River from Washington DC. The announcement inaccurately describes the design as a "double helix" but scholars of ancient history and the Bible will readily recognize the ancient model for the design: the Tower of Babel...

Construction on their second corporate headquarters is expected to begin next year and when completed in 2025 at a cost of $2.5 billion. It will include 2.8 million square feet of new office space distributed across three 22-story buildings. The location is less than four miles from the Capitol Building...

"The natural beauty of a double helix can be seen throughout our world, from the geometry of our own DNA to the elemental form of galaxies, weather patterns, pinecones, and seashells," the company said. "The Helix at our Arlington headquarters will offer a variety of alternative work environments for Amazon employees amidst lush gardens and flourishing trees native to the region."

Though it is true that DNA is arranged in a double-helix, the architectural design is not, in fact, a double helix that appears like a ladder that has been twisted into a corkscrew. The design of the building is, perhaps, a single helix with a spiral walkway ascending the exterior of the building. The architectural design of the Amazon building does, in fact, closely resemble that of a ziggurat, a type of massive structure built in ancient Mesopotamia.

A ziggurat has the form of a terraced compound of successively receding stories or levels.[22]

While America might not be the Babylon of Revelation 18, it more and more looks the part—up to and including the infamous tower God brought crashing down for that people's anti-God rebellion.

Continue to pray things will change, but realize the Lord must judge wickedness:

Righteousness exalteth a nation: but sin is a reproach to any people. (Proverbs 14:34)

The Lord of Heaven is not without complete awareness of His people having to contend with the wickedness all around them. This is why the following verse about that future Babylon of Revelation 18 is a call we of this generation might soon hear from Heaven:

Then I heard another voice from heaven say: "Come out of her, my people, so that you will not share in her sins, so that you will not receive any of her plagues." (Revelation 18:4)

Satan's Prepping and Babel Construction

"Preppers" are sometimes deemed wise, sometimes lauded, and often criticized as conspiracy theorists—and worse. Whatever their acceptance, praise, or condemnation, their very existence and proliferation gives credence, even validation, to their fear that "something wicked this way comes," as Mr. Shakespeare might say. And whether one's a prepper or not, even a non-Bible prophecy observer can recognize growing wickedness in every direction on the cultural and societal landscape.

Prepping, of course, is gathering all sorts of supplies to prepare against hard times to come. Fear is prevalent and growing that there will be a complete fiscal breakdown—that the dollar will massively lose value and be replaced by alternative economic systems worldwide. There is a belief that society will collapse under the despotic hands of tyrants seeking to bring America down. Fear of cyberattacks and even kinetic attacks are on the rise. There is trepidation that things like this are now being planned by the likes of Russia and China against a once well-protected America—a nation no longer secured against such destructive possibilities.

I admit to writing about these fearful prospects, in the context of trying to be discerning about what God's Word has to say about this generation as it approaches the time Jesus said will be the most horrific of human history (Matthew 24:21). So a growing percentage of the earth's inhabitants are looking at what they see coming, and are trying to protect themselves and those they love from a possibly unprecedented assault against humanity. Some are pulling out all stops.

The billionaires we hear about are doing things like buying up old, deserted missile silos and fixing them up for long-term living underground while the chaos of nuclear war and other deadly things occur on the planet's surface. Lesser financially secured folks who are equally apprehensive about things to come are stockpiling foods, medical supplies, and anything else they think would be necessary to survive.

Of course, admittedly, the vast majority of the world's populations, if they think at all about such dire possibilities, do so for only a fleeting moment. They are too busy doing life from one minute to the next.

There is one, however, who is doing a different kind of prepping. And he is doing so at breakneck speed. We can see his handiwork in that regard by simply observing the times and watching headlines unfold. It's as if he knows he has a short time to prepare in consideration of his biblically forecast destiny.

Of course I'm talking about Satan, who is in an all-out phase of prepping, as I believe I and others can discern in these increasingly troublesome times. He has his collars and chains around the necks of the dogs of government, military, economy, science, entertainment, and especially religion.

In government we see developments shaping swiftly into the final, global entity Daniel the prophet spoke of to King Nebuchadnezzar. In military matters, we see war being threatened in areas of prophetic significance. World War III is considered almost a certainty by some of the most revered military affairs experts. In the economy we see developments toward the coming marks-and-number (666) system of Revelation chapter 13. In science, artificial intelligence and all things digital are bringing all of humanity under surveillance and controls that will provide Satan's man, Antichrist, everything he needs to enslave a world—one that obviously is already in a compliant mood to worship Lucifer.

The goings-on during Super Bowl LVII made it clear, at least within the microcosm of that screaming throng, that the masses might be all in on welcoming the coming man of sin and his Beast state. The following *Now the End Begins* article, titled "At Super Bowl Halftime Show, Rihanna Keeps the Satanic Spirit of Last Week's Grammys Alive and Kicking in Demonic Aerial Display with Fallen Angels," was featured in Rapture Ready's news section:

> Last week, we showed you how the Grammys invited to world to enjoy something "beautifully unholy," and then cheered as Satan was prayed to, invoked and worshipped on international

tell-a-vision, and "sponsored by Pfizer" no less. Moments ago, the 2023 Super Bowl Halftime Show opened with filth merchant Rihanna descending from the sky, surrounded by what could only be described as dancing fallen angels, and sang "Bi**h Better Have My Money." What was the reaction? Cheering and applause so loud that it competed with the music for your ear. You can stop having that debate now on whether or not America is a Christian nation, we absolutely are not.[23]

In religion, there is movement of all belief systems attempting to come together as one. Pope Francis is consistently seen at the forefront of the effort while he applauds and approves of the World Economic Forum (WEF) efforts to bring the world back to Babel. We witnessed a meeting on traditional Mount Sinai in Egypt, where globalists came down after visiting the top, bringing down (in a way that mocked God's Ten Commandments) their ten commandments for dealing with climate change and other world problems.

All of this is Satan's prepping. While the world prepares to survive what they fear is coming, the devil is preparing with all at his disposal to bring on that very devastation the human preppers fear.

I believe one of the chief signs we see in Satan's prepping is the activity going on with the unidentified flying objects for which nobody within the military command system seems to have an answer.

The question I have: Is the world, with this sudden rash of UFOs, being further prepared to accept a space-brother-visitation explanation for that stunning moment when the Rapture occurs? This sudden phenomenon, in conjunction with the insanity being perpetrated against children, gives reason for wonder.

We can expect Satan's building-back-Babel prepping to become more intensive as time passes. Perhaps part of the reason Jesus told us to keep looking up is that Satan's prepping—the so-called UFOs, etc—will be a key indicator of the Lord's very soon call to believers:

And when these things begin to come to pass, then look up, and lift up your heads; for your redemption draweth nigh. (Luke 21: 28)

Wondrous Woman's Midnight Ride

Perhaps the strangest of the nearing-midnight prophetic signals to consider is the prophecy about the woman who rides the beast (Revelation 17). In his 2005 book, A *Woman Rides the Beast*, my friend, prophecy expert Dave Hunt, examined this almost dumbfounding foretelling. It is dumbfounding, at least, to those who make little effort to understand— or even believe—things written in the prophetic books of God's Word.

The world as a whole today is as clueless as ever, even though tremendous stage-setting for bringing forth the woman who will ride the beast cannot be missed by those spiritually attuned to issues and events of the day. One clear manifestation of humans wanting to build back Babel and things taking place for bringing about John's Patmos vision played before all the eyes of the world in an Olympic Games opening ceremony not long ago.

All the beautiful pageantry was there. Excitement and joy were on the faces of the colorfully clad athletes from around the globe. The world's media focused its attention on how wonderful it was that the two Korean youths were marching together and getting along as if peace and love had overruled hatred and division—all in all, a kumbaya moment in the 2018 Winter Olympic Games.

Not far into the ceremony, a familiar anthem to the brotherhood of man swept everyone involved into a euphoric high. The music invited us all to imagine all the world as one.

Neo-Babel builders construct even their music in a way that clearly demonstrates the Luciferian desire to usurp God's throne. John Lennon's universally popular song, "Imagine," could easily be mistaken as portraying the biblically prophesied Millennial Reign of Jesus Christ. But John Lennon, like Vladimir Lenin, preached man-made heaven on earth—a mockery of the true Messiah's coming Kingdom. The words and melody many of us know by heart are infectious.

Lennon, who once assured us that the Beatles were "bigger than Jesus Christ," is a bit off in his assessment given through his lyrics. He says "no religion, too." He wanted us to "imagine" a world without religious restraint. Only then could we all "be as one."

That sentiment—"no religion, too"—will have to be rewritten if it is to fit what's coming when the first and second beasts of Revelation bring their version of Heaven on earth to the planet.

It will be an intrusive religious system:

> So he carried me away in the spirit into the wilderness: and I saw a woman sit upon a scarlet colored beast, full of names of blasphemy, having seven heads and ten horns. And the woman was arrayed in purple and scarlet colour, and decked with gold and precious stones and pearls, having a golden cup in her hand full of abominations and filthiness of her fornication: And upon her forehead was a name written, Mystery, Babylon the Great, the Mother of Harlots and Abominations of the Earth. And I saw the woman drunken with the blood of the saints, and with the blood of the martyrs of Jesus: and when I saw her, I wondered with great admiration. (Revelation 17:3–6)

The angel who showed John the Revelator these things said this whorish woman who rides the beast sits upon seven mountains or hills. The beast she rides is a composite of world kingdoms of the past and one yet to come. The last kingdom and the one who rules it will be Antichrist.

We know from Revelation 13 that his sidekick will be the False Prophet—a religious leader who will orchestrate the worldwide worship of this eighth king who will come up from the bottomless pit.

All of this said, it's more than interesting that the world's most lauded religious leader in Christendom has weighed in on how America needs to be brought under the world community's control if there is to be Heaven on earth at any time in the future.

Pope Francis told the Italian newspaper *La Repubblica* that the United States of America has "a distorted vision of the world" and Americans must be ruled by a world government as soon as possible, "for their own good."

The pope made the observation in an interview with journalist Eugenio Scalfari.

"Last Thursday, I got a call from Pope Francis," Scalfari reported. "It was about noon, and I was at the newspaper when my phone rang."

He said Pope Francis had been watching Putin and Trump at the G20 intergovernmental forum and had become agitated. The pope demanded to see the reporter at four that afternoon, according to a Google translation of the Italian report.

"Pope Francis told me to be very concerned about the meeting of the G20," Scalfari wrote.

As translated into English by Agence France Presse (AFP), which picked up the story, the pope said, "I am afraid there are very dangerous alliances between powers who have a distorted view of the world: America and Russia, China and North Korea, Russia and Assad in the war in Syria."

"The danger concerns immigration," the pope continued to *La Repubblica*. "Our main and unfortunately growing problem in the world today is that of the poor, the weak, the excluded, which includes migrants."

"This is why the G20 worries me: It mainly hits immigrants," Pope Francis said, according to AFP.

Pope Francis' idea that Americans would be better off under a world government doesn't stop there. The radical leftist pontiff also went on record stating that Europe should become one country under one government.[24]

As we near the midnight of world history on God's prophetic clock, we see the four horsemen of Apocalypse getting set to ride. Might we be seeing the woman that rides the beast of Revelation chapter 17 getting ready to sit upon its back?

11

Demonic Descent

WHEN I FIRST READ THE HEADLINE to the story, a laugh spilled from my mouth automatically, almost as did the coffee I was drinking. It was at first glance a knee-slapper. But the gravity of the truth within the article drew my attention more deeply.

The headline stated: "House Chaplain Casts Out Demons During Morning Prayer in Capitol Building."

My first thought was: *If he exorcised all the demons weaving their way in and out of the House of Representatives in Washington, DC, there might not be enough of that body left to conduct government business.* That's not, perhaps, a kind way to think of our elected representatives. But with the things going on there and in and around all of what has come to be called the "swamp," my instantaneous take on that headline seemingly is justifiable.

This is the gist of the story:

Reverend Patrick Conroy serves as the House of Representatives Chaplain in Washington, D.C. and regularly starts the day off for lawmakers with prayer.

Thursday's invocation was a little more serious than most days for Rev. Conroy. The Roman Catholic Priest prayed specifically to cast out the demons inside Capitol Hill.

As reported by Fox News, Rev. Conroy said, "This has been a difficult and contentious week in which darker spirits seem to have been at play in the people's House."

"Then, in a dramatic moment, Conroy raised both hands and said, 'In Your most holy name, I cast out all spirits of darkness from this chamber. Spirits not from You. I cast out the spirit of discouragement which deadens the hope of those who are of goodwill.'"

"I cast out the spirit of petty divisiveness which clouds the sense and the desire to be of fruitful productivity and addressing the issues more appropriately before this House," he prayed. "I cast out any sadness brought on by the frustration of dealing with matters detrimental to the honorable work each member has been called to engage in."

Rev. Conroy is a Jesuit priest, an order of the Catholic Church. He has been serving as House Chaplain since 2011.[25]

I don't mean to make fun of this gentleman's desire or attempts to cast out the dark spirits from the House of Representatives. But, if it had happened in actuality, I believe there would have been an audible swooshing not unlike the sound made by a vacuum cleaner. I can say this with a degree of certainty because our congressional bodies are considered the highest levels, in human terms, of powers and principalities.

Here, again, is what God's Word, through the Apostle Paul, has to say about this very matter of dark spirits and high places.

> For we wrestle not against flesh and blood, but against principalities, against powers, against the rulers of the darkness of this world, against spiritual wickedness in high places. (Ephesians 6:12)

Such august human political, religious, and educational bodies are where these minions reside in great numbers. Their human consorts too often do their bidding, and we certainly are witnessing as never before the activities of these powers and principalities in high places.

In my opinion, we can sense the evil, bony fingers of these dark entities manipulating their congressional human pawns. For example, the four freshmen Democratic House members—who, when they were new in office, termed themselves "the Squad"—led the way in taking that party ever farther from common sensibility and morality so long associated with American comportment.

One of the four in particular continues to exhibit a virulent hatred for the nation of Israel. She did so even under pressure not to by such powerful people as House Speaker Nancy Pelosi. Rep. Ilhan Omar (D-MN), a Muslim, refuses to back off her angry statements condemning all Jews and Israel. At the same time, she and the other three members of the Squad want to destroy America as founded and replace it with their vision of a socialist utopia.

The former Democratic majority in the House of Representatives, led, in effect, by Millennial types such as these four anti-America-as-founded women, seek to bring minuscule minority elements such as LGBTQ+ and others dedicated to doing away with moral restraint to the forefront of governing the culture. They intend to make the perversions that used to be unmentionable in public the new norm for life in America.

The Squad has stood with great applause in adulation over their fellow party members making it legal in several states to murder babies right after birth. This is done all for the woman's right to choose who lives and dies. There is now movement afoot among these same congressional types to make euthanasia legal in cases of the elderly and infirm.

And these very minions of the dark powers and principalities have the audacity to accuse this president and those who support him of being Nazis, because they want to bring America back to its founding principles.

The Lord now has the evil leaders in derision, as He states in Psalm 2. While I can't say I go along with either the Catholic idea of practicing Christianity or with their view of exorcising evil spirits, I'm with this chaplain in wishing to cast out those powers and principalities.

Again, we are told to "stand" in these evil, closing days of the age, and we're instructed how to spiritually dress in order to "stand" against our opposition:

> Wherefore take unto you the whole armour of God, that ye may be able to withstand in the evil day, and having done all, to stand. Stand therefore, having your loins girt about with truth, and having on the breastplate of righteousness; and your feet shod with the preparation of the gospel of peace; above all, taking the shield of faith, wherewith ye shall be able to quench all the fiery darts of the wicked. And take the helmet of salvation, and the sword of the Spirit, which is the word of God: Praying always with all prayer and supplication in the Spirit, and watching thereunto with all perseverance and supplication for all saints. (Ephesians 6:13–18)

Pre-Trib Portals

My attention is incessantly drawn to the increasing wickedness that, within just the past few years, seems to have invaded our reality. Nothing now seems to be as near to "normal" as things were, say, in 2020.

My own human thoughts interject that it's because my ninety-seven-year-old mom died early that year. Her passing made everything darker because I lost the Lord's brightness within her that had illuminated my path. She gave me my Scripture for life, written in the front leaf of the Bible she gave me when I was very young:

> Trust in the lord with all thine heart, and lean not unto thine own understanding. In all thy ways acknowledge him and he shall direct thy paths. (Proverbs 3:5–6)

Forgetting for a brief time to use that biblical flashlight Mom had handed me as a youngster, during the natural mourning process when she passed away, things did *not* look to be as they had been before.

But that other light within (the Holy Spirit, not my human thoughts) soon reminded me of the Proverbs 3:5–6 truth—the light Kathleen James-Basse left behind in February 2020, when Heaven became brighter than ever.

So, it isn't anything personal affecting my life that gives this world a sense of increased strangeness and malevolence. There is most definitely a supernatural aura about life today that wasn't there before—and it's not from the good side of that other dimension.

My attention is incessantly drawn to the increasing wickedness that seems to have within just the past few years invaded our reality, because the Holy Spirit prompts my spirit to sense that there is indeed an invasion taking place. The other dimension this invasion is coming from is what I call "pre-Trib portals."

I use this term because the demonic activity that God's Word says will prevail during the Tribulation seems to already be seeping, maybe more like flooding, into our reality even now. Therefore, there is a pre-Trib intrusion into our time before the Rapture of the Church. This, I'm convinced, is all in preparation for the Antichrist's regime of horror Jesus said will bring forth the worst period of human history (Matthew 24:21). Satan is trying to set the stage upon which his son of perdition will step when believers are taken off the earth and the "covenant with many" of Daniel chapter 9 is confirmed by "the prince that shall come."

In America, this preparation has been taking place for many decades. I believe it began in earnest shortly after the start of the twentieth century. It has accelerated swiftly and is now at full throttle.

My friend Michael Hile, in an article, presented a record of this invasion through the pre-Trib portals. When the nation, through court action, began removing God and His righteous principles for life from the national conscience, the vacuum created a supernatural opening for the invading forces from the dark side. Here's what Michael wrote:

The United States has been in a moral freefall that accelerated in the decade of the '60s with restrictions on prayer (1962) and

Bible reading in the public schools (1963). The U.S. Supreme Court has systematically helped destroy religious liberty in America with the following 12 court cases:

- 1925: The Scopes "Monkey" trial—*Tennessee v. Scopes,* https://en.wikipedia.org/wiki/Scopes_Trial
- 1940: The Free Exercise Clause is created—*Cantwell v. Connecticut,* https://en.wikipedia.org/wiki/Cantwell_v._Connecticut
- 1947: The Establishment Clause is created—*Everson v. Board of Education,* https://en.wikipedia.org/wiki/Everson_v._Board_of_Education
- 1962: Prayer is removed from the schools—*Engel v. Vitale,* https://en.wikipedia.org/wiki/Engel_v._Vitale
- 1963: Bible reading is removed from the schools— *Abington School District v. Schempp,* https://en.wikipedia.org/wiki/Abington_School_District_v._Schempp
- 1973: The murder of unborn babies is legalized—*Roe v. Wade,* https://en.wikipedia.org/wiki/Roe_v._Wade
- 1980: The Ten Commandments are removed from school classrooms—*Stone v. Graham,* https://en.wikipedia.org/wiki/Stone_v._Graham
- 1992: Invocations/benedictions are banned from school activities—*Lee v. Weisman,* https://en.wikipedia.org/wiki/Lee_v._Weisman
- 2003: Sodomy is legalized by the Supreme Court— *Lawrence v. Texas,* https://en.wikipedia.org/wiki/Lawrence_v._Texas
- 2005: Display of the Ten Commandments is ruled unconstitutional—*McCreary County v. ACLU of Kentucky,* https://en.wikipedia.org/wiki/McCreary_County_v._American_Civil_Liberties_Union

- 2013: Defense of Marriage Act is declared unconstitutional—*United States v. Windsor,* https://en.wikipedia.org/wiki/United_States_v._Windsor
- 2015: Same-sex marriage is approved by the Supreme Court—*Obergefell v. Hodges,* https://en.wikipedia.org/wiki/Obergefell_v._Hodges[26]

The evil being directed at children is perhaps the most significant manifestation of what is pouring through the pre-Trib portals. It is concentrated wickedness, and even parents of the children seem to have lost spiritual immunity to Satan's deadly venom.

Proof that America has reached the reprobate mindset of Romans 1:28 is clearly shown, I think, through the opinion on children rendered by the top leader in America—the leadership position once considered the highest in the free world:

Monday's segment of Comedy Central's *The Daily Show*, President Joe Biden spoke with gay man and former White House staff member in the Obama era, Kal Penn, where he admitted that he thought restricting kids from getting their private parts mutilated was "sinful."...

"Transgender kids is a really harder thing," he began. "What's going on in Florida is, as my mother would say, close to sinful. I mean it's terrible what they're doing."

In Florida, Governor Ron DeSantis is spearheading laws that would prohibit kids from receiving dangerous surgeries and drugs to change their gender. DeSantis recognizes that there are two genders and that children are not mature enough to make such life altering decisions. While his laws are evidence of him looking out for children's best interests, the left is twisting it into an anti-LGBTQ campaign by the Republican Governor...

Regardless, Biden insisted that he was looking to pass legislation that would allow transgender youth to harm their bodies and added, "You mess with that, you're breaking the law, and you're gonna be held accountable."

It really is a shame that Biden is using his platform and position of power to facilitate such a grave evil in this nation. Kids need to be protected, not infected by the disease of the woke left.[27]

With such upside-down declaration, can there be any doubt that the pre-Trib portals are as wide open as America's southern borders?

The CCP Techno-Demons

If you've been keeping up with what's going on in the science of artificial intelligence (AI), you're aware that the bite into the fruit of the tree of the knowledge of good and evil is again taking place. The present-day satanic tempters are not whispering into the ears of humankind, but are blatantly and proudly pronouncing that we can and will become like God if we partake of the technological breakthroughs.

The term "transhumanism" was obviously formed in the rebellious brilliance of Lucifer's own mind. The term carries a promise that we can one day be like gods. We will not surely die. We will be like the "most High" and live eternally through the transformation.

It seems that with each news cycle, new frontiers have been pierced while those devoted to AI and transhumanism rage to bring about Heaven on earth totally apart from God. It is in this rage that the devil and his demonic agents might be laying plans to bring about the demise of much of humankind.

Almost certainly, these new technologies have been inspired by such minions. Perhaps it is all setting up to fulfill Bible prophecy, particularly in an area I would like us to consider here briefly.

No geopolitical force on earth at present is more determined than the Chinese Communist Party (CCP) to involve all of humanity in a tyrannical way. And, it is with some imagination that I speculate a bit on how this most wicked geopolitical agency of the Oriental world will be inspired to use the technologies I believed are spawned from the mind of the fallen one.

News over the past few years gives credence to my thinking in this regard. For example:

> The U.S. military's top intelligence officer is increasingly worried about China's research into "human performance enhancement," including efforts to merge human and machine intelligence.
>
> It's a "key area" of disruptive technology that will affect national security, Lt. Gen. Robert Ashley, the director of the Defense Intelligence Agency, or DIA, told an audience at the Association of the U.S. Army's annual conference this week.
>
> Chinese efforts to teach machines to think—through emerging technologies like neural nets, a form of artificial intelligence—represent phases of a process that concludes with "the next step, the integration of human and machines," Ashley said. This, he said, could result in "cognitive advances not just in how we think, but [also] think about the stamina of the individual soldier; think about the ethical impacts of those kind of technologies and how they would be applied? And how does a democracy view those type of technologies? How will Russia and China leverage those?"
>
> [Elsa Kania, a fellow with the Technology and National Security Program at the Center for a New American Security,] wrote in an email. "The PLA's Academy of Military Science has focused on advancing military-civil fusion (or civil-military integration, 军民融合) in brain science research, including to explore options to enhance human capabilities for battlefield perception and decision-making."
>
> That includes everything from implants that enable human

wetware (brains) to interact with and share digital information with hardware (computers), to gene-editing through tools like CRISPR. Such work may one day allow China to grow superior troops, or turn regular soldiers into super ones.[28]

Here is the prophecy about the immense destructive power of the kings of the east:

> Saying to the sixth angel which had the trumpet, Loose the four angels which are bound in the great river Euphrates. And the four angels were loosed, which were prepared for an hour, and a day, and a month, and a year, for to slay the third part of men. And the number of the army of the horsemen were two hundred thousand thousand: and I heard the number of them.... By these three was the third part of men killed, by the fire, and by the smoke, and by the brimstone, which issued out of their mouths. (Revelation 9:14–16, 18)

The warning of this great force from the Oriental world is further expounded upon in the following passage:

> And the sixth angel poured out his vial upon the great river Euphrates; and the water thereof was dried up, that the way of the kings of the east might be prepared. And I saw three unclean spirits like frogs come out of the mouth of the dragon, and out of the mouth of the beast, and out of the mouth of the false prophet. For they are the spirits of devils, working miracles, which go forth unto the kings of the earth and of the whole world, to gather them to the battle of that great day of God Almighty. (Revelation 16:12–14)

While it is speculation that the AI and transhumanistic "science" of today might bid the entrance of demons from beneath the dried-up

Euphrates, my thoughts are based upon scriptural integrity. There are accounts of demons inhabiting human beings throughout the Bible. It is forbidden, as given in Deuteronomy, for instance, to summon spirits, etc. Clearly these developing technologies might give an opening for those entities described as having been incarcerated beneath the Euphrates region.

With all areas of earth's tumult shaping up for the soon fulfillment of end-times prophecy, the growing power of the CCP and their devotion to AI and transhumanism in order to enhance their military capability makes them look more and more like the kings of the east. This horrendous offspring of the world's most prolific mass murderer, Mao Zedong, is scheduled to be demon possessed as a two hundred million-strong juggernaut. They will murder billions with their power.

But it's not yet time for such domination and destructiveness.

No matter how frightening the prospects might be for those who look in growing fear of the CCP and its threat, we can take comfort. God is still in absolute control. He will take His own to safety before that great and terrible day of the Lord.

The earth is the Lord's, and the fullness thereof; the world, and they that dwell therein. For he hath founded it upon the seas, and established it upon the floods. Who shall ascend into the hill of the Lord? or who shall stand in his holy place? He that hath clean hands, and a pure heart; who hath not lifted up his soul unto vanity, nor sworn deceitfully. He shall receive the blessing from the Lord, and righteousness from the God of his salvation. (Psalms 24:1–5)

12

Discerning the Midnight Hour

Author's note: The following is taken in part from my conclusion in the book Discerners: Analyzing Converging Prophetic Signs for the End of Days.

OUR WEEKLY COLUMN on the raptureready.com website is called "Nearing Midnight" because we discern that the earth has almost reached the midnight hour of the Church Age, also called the Age of Grace.

Whereas the geopolitical, humanist powers that be frame their view of human history's closing minutes within their doomsday clock, we observe these fleeting times before Christ's call to the Church by placing the template of Bible prophecy over the converging of prophetic stage-setting.

Political scientists and other scientists can only guess at what will happen to the human race. Most all believe that humankind will meet its end from nuclear holocaust or by climate-change disasters.

We can know for certain, through a detailed preview by God, Himself, how the end of all things will unfold. We don't know precisely *when* the end will come. We know, however, the *general time* it will begin to manifest—when the "midnight hour" of God's prophetic timeline is approaching.

The Lord Jesus gave born-again believers explicit instructions about how and when to discern the nearing midnight hour:

And when you see all these things begin to come to pass, then look up, and lift up your head, for your redemption draws near. (Luke 21: 28)

Note that Jesus didn't say to watch for when these things "come to pass." He said "when these things *begin* to come to pass," we are to "look up and lift up our heads," for our "redemption is drawing near" (Luke 21:28). At that time, He will be on His way to rescue His Bride (the Church) from the carnage about to take place on earth.

The blackness of the midnight hour will descend following that rescue of the Church. Seven years into the Tribulation, complete evil will have engulfed the planet with satanic darkness. The first bright gleaming to pierce that horrendous time will then burst through the billowing storm clouds of Armageddon. Brilliant light will part the heavens, and Christ and His army will appear.

So, understanding the times in which we find ourselves is all-important. If it was not possible to discern the times, Jesus wouldn't have told us: "What I say unto one, I say unto all. Watch" (Mark 13:37). He promises in Revelation 3:10 that we are not appointed to God's wrath, and will be kept out of the very time of that wrath.

So, what did the Lord say would be taking place—the things "beginning to come to pass" that we see happening at this very moment? Exactly *what* are the things for which we are to look?

Remember, the whole Bible is the *Word* of God. And, Jesus is that *Word* (John 1:1). Every prophecy, whether it's already accomplished or yet to be fulfilled, is attributable to Him. God, the Holy Spirit, inspired the Old and New Testament prophets to give the prophecies. So, we don't have to consider just what the Lord Jesus said by way of prophecy to discern the times in which we live. We must consider every prophecy yet to be fulfilled, presented in the Bible by all Bible prophets.

I believe we are seeing the *stage being set* for fulfillment of prophecy yet future rather than *fulfillment* itself. The one caveat concerns the nation of

Israel. Israel again being a nation after millennia of dispersion into all the world is fulfilled prophecy.

That said, however, everything we see happening around us at this very hour has prophetic significance. Some things are profoundly significant—for example, the coalition of nations forming to Israel's north.

Russia (the land of Magog), Iran (much of ancient Persia), and Turkey (the land of Togarmah) coming together in a coalescing alliance is a spectacular example of God's knowledge of things to come. These, of course, are exactly the central actors prophetically scheduled to come against God's chosen nation, Israel, according to Ezekiel 38 and 39.

It must be agreed that much of the stage-setting itself is likened to fulfilled prophecy in some ways. For example, the Apostle Paul's "perilous times" words presented in 2 Timothy 3 offer a vivid snapshot of these spiritually darkening days. While prophecy yet future, for the most part, seems to be reserved for the Tribulation (Daniel's seventieth week), developments in our nation and world are becoming ever more like those outlined in God's Word for that last seven years immediately preceding Christ's Second Advent.

Luciferic darkening has so infected this generation in America and throughout the world that we who "watch" in order to discern the times are brought face-to-face with end-times insanity born of greatly increased rebellion against God. Other than the fact that Israel itself is what most view as the most dramatic sign of where this generation stands on God's prophetic timeline, there runs a deadly septicemia throughout humankind that marks this as a generation at the very end of its prophetic rope. The infection proves we are in the terminal stage of rebellion.

Paul explains very clearly that infection, satanically injected into humanity's bloodstream:

For the wrath of God is revealed from heaven against all ungodliness and unrighteousness of men, who hold the truth in unrighteousness; because that which may be known of God is manifest in them; for God hath shewed it unto them. For the invisible things of him from the creation of the world are clearly seen, being understood by the things that are made, even his eternal power and Godhead; so that they are without excuse: Because that, when they knew God, they glorified him not as God, neither were thankful; but became vain in their imaginations, and their foolish heart was darkened. Professing themselves to be wise, they became fools, and changed the glory of the uncorruptible God into an image made like to corruptible man, and to birds, and fourfooted beasts, and creeping things.

Wherefore God also gave them up to uncleanness through the lusts of their own hearts, to dishonour their own bodies between themselves: Who changed the truth of God into a lie, and worshipped and served the creature more than the Creator, who is blessed for ever. Amen. For this cause God gave them up unto vile affections: for even their women did change the natural use into that which is against nature: And likewise also the men, leaving the natural use of the woman, burned in their lust one toward another; men with men working that which is unseemly, and receiving in themselves that recompence of their error which was meet. And even as they did not like to retain God in their knowledge, God gave them over to a reprobate mind, to do those things which are not convenient; being filled with all unrighteousness, fornication, wickedness, covetousness, maliciousness; full of envy, murder, debate, deceit, malignity; whisperers, backbiters, haters of God, despiteful, proud, boasters, inventors of evil things, disobedient to parents, without understanding, covenantbreakers, without natural affection, implacable, unmerciful: Who knowing the judgment of God, that they which commit such things are worthy of death, not only do the same, but have pleasure in them that do them. (Romans 1:18–32)

God condemns those who are caught in this destructive quagmire of depravity. But Jesus gives us the way out of that soul-destroying quicksand:

> Verily, verily, I say unto you, He that heareth my word, and believeth on him that sent me, hath everlasting life, and shall not come into condemnation; but is passed from death unto life. (John 5:24)

Discerning the Right/Wrong Side of Things

Discerning the lateness of the prophetic hour is the Holy Spirit's gift to each believer who seeks such insight. It is not only the privilege given by the Holy Spirit, however. It is the responsibility of believers to understand the lateness of the hour in which we find ourselves.

There is no more profound indicator of exactly where this generation stands on God's prophetic timeline than the political machinations of today.

There is talk in every political season of one "litmus test" or another. In other words, in order to get the endorsement of one faction or another, candidates must show—through a litmus test—that they support the programs, platforms, and proposals of those whose endorsements they seek.

For example, to be accepted by today's Democratic Party, candidates must get behind a woman's right to choose. That is, they have to totally embrace abortion at the level the Democratic Party champions. If prospective contenders go against this or any other litmus test, they can forget getting anywhere so far as electability is concerned.

The Democratic Party's rules committee determines who is "right" or "wrong" in this sense. One is determined to be on the "right" or "wrong" side of any given issue by what is considered acceptable ideology or viewpoint by the party's rules. By this process, candidates are accepted or rejected as worthy or not.

The Democratic Party has been shown to support abortion, LGTBQ+ issues, open borders, sanctuary cities, the anti-Second Amendment right to have and bear arms, anti-law enforcement issues, anti-Israel proposals and actions, and other such propositions that directly oppose conservative Christian views.

Democratic positions are considered on the left side of the political spectrum. That is, they are liberal or progressive in their ideological leanings. In these hyper-charged days in regard to politics, the views held by the Democratic Party are ultra-leftist in the view of most who want to maintain traditional American values—i.e., those generally held sacred since the nation's founding.

Those of us with traditional American values are considered to be on the political right. The leftists consider us radical right-wingers.

I agree that we who hold to the common-sense side of things in the world of culture and society are right. And those on the left are wrong. They're not wrong because I say so, or because the US Constitution says so. They're wrong because God's Word says so.

A book I wrote several years ago with sixteen other authors laid out the case for discerning right and wrong from God's unerring perspective. *Discerners: Analyzing Converging Prophetic Signs for the End of Days* covers many of the wrong issues assaulting our nation and world today.

Discernment is not an option for Christians. Jesus told every believer who would come down through the ages: "What I say unto one, I say unto all. Watch" (Mark 13:37). He was telling those of today who are in the middle of enduring the wrongs being done that we are to see these things and understand how near He is to coming back to rectify those wrongs. We are to know the times and seasons. This is a commandment, not a request.

We know right and wrong by comparing the things going on around us to what the Bible says about them. In the case of the issues championed by the leftists as given above, we, as Christians are to be shrewd. We are to examine each issue and compare it to God's Holy Word to determine whether the issue is right or wrong.

Let's do so to just a few of the things the political left champions.

Abortion

The progressive/left side of the political spectrum has championed this travesty that has killed more than sixty million babies in their mothers' wombs since 1973. They now, by and large, support the killing of a baby who survives the attempted abortion. They have seen to it that the right to carry out this grisly process has legal backing in a growing number of places. God's Holy Word says shedding the blood of the innocent is something He hates (see, for example, Proverbs 6:16, 17).

LGTBQ+

The progressive/left fully backs the LGTBQ+ and all that organized, anti-God coalition ravenously pursues. They demand that males can love males and females can love females in the romantic or sexual way without consequence or judgment from God or anyone else. They proclaim that marriage between the same sexes is the moral equivalent of heterosexual marriage. They declare that all have the right to become a gender other than that with which they were born. It is their choice, not that of any religious entity of any sort.

The Bible says it is an abomination for man to lie with a man and woman with a woman. It is a most egregious sin in God's Holy eyes. His Word says He created man and woman, male and female. He ordained one man and one woman to be together in marriage for life.

Anti-Israel Proposals and Actions

The most prominent prophetic sign that lets discerning Christians know where this generation stands is the nation Israel. That nation—the Jewish people—contrasts starkly against the darkening backdrop of these last days. Israel and the world's treatment of it demonstrate clearly that the time of Christ's return must be very near.

There is a growing denial, even in the evangelical church, that today's

Israel is a nation blessed by God to be His chosen people. This lie is from the pit. Read Romans 11 to get the absolute truth about God's heart for this people. That heavenly embrace will never change!

This doesn't mean today's Jewish people are perfect. They are far from it. In fact, they are in total spiritual blindness, Scripture tells us.

This is yet another confirmation from Bible prophecy that we are at the end of the Age of Grace. Only a remnant of Israel will ultimately recognize their Messiah—the Lord Jesus Christ—when He returns at Armageddon. Only that remaining group of people will be saved to repopulate the millennial Israel under the throne of David.

Still, they belong to God. Israel is the same Israel of old. God loves them and will move Heaven and Hell during the Tribulation to bring about a remnant who will believe in His Son Jesus as their Messiah.

And Israel is the chief signal by which we can discern what is right and wrong in looking at the political left. Here is a litmus test for you in any political season. There is a disdain for God's chosen nation at the very heart of the Democratic Party. The following news excerpt of several years ago tells the story:

> Not a single 2020 Democrat candidate from the massive field spoke at AIPAC's pro-Israel summit in the spring. But 5 of the 2020 Dems, Sanders, Buttigieg, Castro, Klobuchar, and Bennett, were featured at the J Street conference alongside anti-Israel activists, BDS supporters, and terrorists.
>
> Those 2020 Dems who couldn't attend the anti-Israel hatefest in person sent video messages.
>
> Elizabeth Warren sent in a video message threatening to cut off aid to Israel unless it surrenders to Islamic terrorists. Then she promised to divide Jerusalem, turning half the ancient holy city into a killing ground for the murderous terrorists already occupying Gaza and portions of the West Bank.
>
> Joe Biden, Beto O'Rourke, Marianne Williamson, and even Andrew Yang joined her in sending messages of support and

friendship to the anti-Israel group which has featured BDS supporters and terrorists.

The majority of the 2020 Democrat field has aligned with an anti-Israel organization.[29]

Discernment in today's world is all-important. God's Word is the only measurement that can validate truth:

Thy word is true from the beginning: and every one of thy righteous judgments endureth for ever. (Psalms 119:160)

Acceleration toward Tribulation

In consideration of discernment, we can talk day and night about our time on the planet being like it was during the days of Sodom. We can mull over constantly and consistently that the world is becoming "as one," as John Lennon would have it. That is, the last world empire is forming exactly like Daniel prophesied. The Antichrist kingdom is almost surely forming before our eyes while the minions, both the supernatural and Deep-State types, are coalescing to bring everyone on earth into conformity with their directives.

We can watch while Christianity is being transmorphed by evil forces into something ungodly—changed into the opposite of what God intended. Reprobate thinking, as Paul the apostle pointed out, is the order of the day. Light is called darkness, good is called evil, and there isn't much left of daily life that seems to indicate we're surrounded by sanity.

Yet with all these factors that aggravate us, none points more precisely to where we are than anything to do with Israel.

Just as everything seemed headed in the direction opposite of what Bible prophecy predicts—Israel beginning to benefit from the Trump administration's support—things have again reversed course. Hamas and all the Israel-hating neighbors in that region are again on the attack. Most all nations are again turning their hate-filled glares toward the Jewish state.

Deals are being made again to restore the billions of dollars to Iran and other anti-Israel diabolists taken from them by the Trump government. The sanctions and other restrictions that were just a year or two ago inhibiting Israel's enemies from building arsenals and coalitions against the Middle East's lone democracy now are being taken down.

This reversal must, I think, mean the Lord has taken His hand of restraint somewhat off the entire matter. America, under the Biden administration, looks to be genuinely beginning to *curse* Israel, as opposed to *blessing* that nation when Mr. Trump was in charge.

With that increasing curse has slithered from the darkest abyss the devilish, venomous serpent called anti-Semitism. Just in the past number of months, a growing, gestating process of hatred of the Jewish race has grown into near-1939 levels in some areas of the world—including parts of the United States of America.

It is a sure sign that the Tribulation period, when God will begin pouring wrath on this rebellious world, must be near indeed. Jesus prophesied that this hatred against His people will, in that future era, be far worse than at any time of human history. Let's look again at what He told His disciples on the Mount of Olives that day:

> When ye therefore shall see the abomination of desolation, spoken of by Daniel the prophet, stand in the holy place, (whoso readeth, let him understand:) Then let them which be in Judaea flee into the mountains: Let him which is on the housetop not come down to take any thing out of his house: Neither let him which is in the field return back to take his clothes. And woe unto them that are with child, and to them that give suck in those days! But pray ye that your flight be not in the winter, neither on the sabbath day: For then shall be great tribulation, such as was not since the beginning of the world to this time, no, nor ever shall be. And except those days should be shortened, there should no flesh be saved: but for the elect's sake those days shall be shortened. (Matthew 24:15–22)

The "elect" Jesus was talking about, of course, is Israel, the Jews of the Tribulation period—the time of "Jacob's trouble" (Jeremiah 30:7).

By that time, at three and one-half years into that seven-year period of horror, Antichrist and the whole world will be turned against Israel. God will be issuing His judgment with His wrath, and Antichrist will be waging war to the extent that all biological life on the planet will die if Jesus doesn't stop the carnage. He says He will do so for the "elect's" sake—on behalf of the remnant of Jews at that time.

Jesus was later recorded by Luke as saying that when we see all of these things "begin" to come to pass, we are to look up, because our redemption is drawing near. I believe this is referring to believers of both the pre-Rapture era (Age of Grace) and those who are alive—particularly Jewish believers—at the time of Armageddon and the Second Advent (Revelation 19:11).

Both groups of believers are to be "looking up" for the approaching redemption, who is Jesus Christ!

With regard to this pre-Rapture era, can we discern God's timeline? Can we see this hatred for the Jews "beginning" to come to pass? Has the level of anti-Semitism prophesied for the end of days begun to take place?

I believe so. I believe the hatred for the house of Israel has been gestating within the incubator of barely contained satanic rage. The restraining hand of the Holy Spirit is being lifted to a degree, letting the spiritually attuned see that end-times anti-Semitism as it begins to crawl from that incubator.

One excerpt illustrates things to come in this regard, I think:

The recent wave of anti-Semitic attacks that swept across the US was sparked by the conflict between Israel and Gaza. But the underlying basis of the attacks having nothing to do with Israel was evident on social media in which the message "Hitler was right" peaked.

The conflict between Israel and Gaza led to spike in anti-Semitic attacks.

The ADL [Anti-Defamation League] recently reported that concurrent with the conflict in Israel, acts of harassment and vandalism, and violence surged in cities with large Jewish populations but also in less urban areas. They claimed a 75% increase in anti-Semitism reports to the agency after Israeli-Palestinian fighting began. The figure jumped from 127 incidents in the two weeks prior to fighting to 222 in the two weeks after violence broke out. Though couched in terms of anti-Zionism, previous Israel-Arab conflicts did not generate such a rise in anti-Semitism.

This was most evident on Twitter where variations of the phrase "Hitler was right" were posted more than 17,000 times (according to the Anti-Defamation League) in just a one-week span in May. In addition, the anti-Semitic hashtag #Covid1948 trended on Twitter in several countries, being shared up to 175 times per minute for over four hours on May 13. The hashtag, likening the birth of the state of Israel in 1948 to the COVID-19 virus, was frequently accompanied by blatantly anti-Jewish content

Anti-Semitism is far more prevalent in the US than most people would think. A recent survey by the…ADL, which tracks incidents of anti-Jewish violence and bias, recorded that 63% of American Jews had experienced or witnessed anti-Semitism over the past five years—a marked increase from the 53% of respondents who expressed the same view in last year's ADL survey. 59% of the respondents in the survey said they felt Jews were less safe in the US today than they were a decade ago, while 49% expressed fear of a violent attack at a synagogue.[30]

The profound uptick in anti-Semitism is fodder for Holy Spirit-directed discernment, in my view. It is an undeniable indication that the rage is speeding up. That should inspire us as believers in Jesus Christ to expect at any moment His shout, "Come up here!" (Revelation 4:1).

Section IV

Deliverance

13

Raging toward Reset

EVANGELIST BILLY GRAHAM wrote a book in the 1970s with the title *World Aflame*. The world then, as now, seemed poised to burst into actual flames. The nuclear-war threat was ever-present, and spiritual evil seemed, as now, to be erupting from the very portal of Hell.

However, that earlier time, in contrast to the extremely troubling things transpiring today, seems almost a pleasant reminiscence to indulge in. But at the same time, it seems that, although things on the horizon are far more volatile than in the year of the release of that book by Dr. Graham, earth's inhabitants scarcely notice the true nature of the dangers we face.

Those who do recognize the true nature of the peril are in the almost infinitesimal minority. While I'm aware this observation no doubt might appear arrogant, it is nonetheless a fact.

Only those who believe in Jesus Christ for salvation can truly grasp the reality of what's coming. And only a tiny minority of those born-again folks understands what's happening while the world and the nation "rage toward reset," as phrased in the title of this chapter.

This end-times generation sits upon an incendiary surface, beneath which are tectonic Tribulation pressures that are about to explode in the most catastrophic eruption of all human history.

Jesus put it this way:

For then shall be great tribulation, such as was not since the beginning of the world to this time, no, nor ever shall be. (Matthew 24:21)

The Tribulation is observably on the brink of erupting, and only the minority of God's eternal family alive at this moment knows and understands the extent of the dangers that are poised to make the planet Hell on earth.

Indeed, the powers and principalities against whom we struggle are deep into preparations for bringing that condition about. The evil, supernatural minions are implementing the chief perpetrator's design to make the earth an inferno of death and destruction. At the same time, the *human* minions—at least, many of them—believe they are creating a utopian world in which they can become as gods. This will require certain circumstances and events to take place. These things are within the Luciferian blueprint, but the human minions believe the blueprint is of their own creation. At least some of this human element within the Ephesians 6:12 cabal believe they are doing God's work—assuming at least a few believe there is a God.

The blueprint is titled the "Great Reset," and the slogan for this scheme for constructing a new version of Babel's tower is "Build Back Better!" The chief human architect for the Great Reset project apparently is Klaus Schwab. This globalist adherent to the Build Back Better mantra framed the neo-Babel building project a few years ago.

In June 2020, Schwab, founder and executive chairman of the World Economic Forum (WEF), presented the plan. He wrote that the COVID-19 lockdowns "may be gradually easing, but anxiety about the world's social and economic prospects is only intensifying." He warned that a "sharp economic downturn has already begun, and we could be facing the worst depression since the 1930s."

"To achieve a better outcome," Schwab continued, "the world must act jointly and swiftly to revamp all aspects of our societies and economies, from education to social contracts and working conditions.

"Every country, from the United States to China, must participate, and every industry, from oil and gas to tech, must be transformed. In short, we need a 'Great Reset' of capitalism."

The following describes the unsavory project from the non-delusional perspective.

This will be your future if some powerful people at the World Economic Forum get their way: you'll own nothing and "be happy about it."

Energy will be green, rationed, and expensive, and travel will be restricted.

Your diet will be controlled, and currency will be digital.

This left-wing dystopian dream is called the Great Reset, and you're supposed to be excited about it.

The Great Reset has been labeled a conspiracy theory and parts of it sound like a conspiracy theory, but everything we know about it comes from the global elites themselves, who have been quite open about it.

"This is not a conspiracy theory. This is a well-documented movement among many of the world's most powerful people," says Justin Haskins, the Editorial Director at The Heartland Institute and a leading authority on the Great Reset. "Fundamentally, this is a radical and complete transformation of everything that we do in our society," Haskins adds. "It will change the way businesses are evaluated, it will coerce businesses to pursue left-wing causes."

The Great Reset was unveiled at the World Economic Forum in Davos, Switzerland, where many of the world's most powerful people go to offer solutions to the world's problems. They have said that the coronavirus pandemic as a historic opportunity to change the way the world operates.

A World Economic Forum video warns, "Right now we're facing a crisis of international proportions. It's going to have a long-term impact on us."

And their solution is essentially global socialism. Think of the Green New Deal combined with the COVID-19 lockdown restrictions and throw in something called the Fourth Industrial Revolution, in which technology is supposed to radically change the way we live and work.

Klaus Schwab, the founder of the World Economic Forum, says the Fourth Industrial Revolution will lead to "a fusion of our physical, our digital and our biological identities."[31]

Those who believe God's prophetic Word recognize the Great Reset as Satan's plan for bringing the Antichrist regime to power. The rage toward "reset" will be pre-empted by Christ's call to all who believe in Him for Salvation. It is the pre-Trib view of Bible prophecy that provides full enlightenment—a more complete understanding of what happens next.

We are *nearing midnight* in ways that are visible in every direction. The true Great Reset is about to be implemented. That will be God's fulfillment of the ultimate promise to all believers who have lived during the Church Age:

> For the Lord himself shall descend from heaven with a shout, with the voice of the archangel, and with the trump of God: and the dead in Christ shall rise first: Then we which are alive and remain shall be caught up together with them in the clouds, to meet the Lord in the air: and so shall we ever be with the Lord. Wherefore comfort one another with these words. (1 Thessalonians 4:16–18)

The Devil in the Digital Details

While this generation rages toward the globalist reset and nears the midnight of this fleeting age, every tick of the second hand of God's prophetic watch gives warning that time is running out and heavenly intervention against the wickedness saturating the planet is imminent.

Tick... Deceivers seek to pull all of humanity away from the truth regarding the God of Creation. The drive is incessant to convince everyone that humans aren't the creation of a deity, but of a primordial accident. The specious science called *evolution* long ago imprinted in people's minds that humankind has struggled up the chain of transition to become Homo sapiens. The most recent outcome of the struggle is that the transition now means women can choose to be men and men can become women merely by saying so. The ongoing transition that denies any involvement with deity has allowed for adults to interact sexually with the youngest children. Parents, many believe, should stay out of the process of the transition taking place. Homosexuality, like in the days of Lot in Sodom, is the overriding societal and cultural new norm the government should protect above all other considerations.

Tick... A stream of monetary greed and vicious militancy flows just beneath the surface of the pseudo-peace that politicians who govern around the world pretend to want to maintain. Rumors of nuclear war inundate our eyes and ears from news feeds hourly. Actual war is ratcheting up in the most dangerous areas that could any moment break into nuclear conflict. Ukraine and all the territories surrounding Israel could become kinetic fields of battle at any moment.

Tick... Religiously, the world is shaping up just as Jesus prophesied. False prophets are arising, even among the most evangelical, fundamentalist ministries. Some teach the Bible is no longer relevant because times have changed. The pope declares there is no literal Hell—there is only Heaven, and its inhabitants will include atheists. Even the dictator of Russia points out the apostasy and evil of religious leaders of the West. And his words are true.

Tick... Technology has developed to the point that it's now possible, according to the anti-God scientists supposedly in the know, to accomplish the total transition of humans. The melding of AI with humans will increase our achievement capacity to a god-like status. Further breakthroughs in computer and biological interactions promise it is possible to eventually bring about something approaching eternal life. Humanity—at least those who fall victim to this line of belief—thus succumb to the serpent's lie to Eve: "You will be as god."

Tick… It now looks as if Satan has brought to the cusp of implementation the system of control God's Word describes in Revelation:

> And he causeth all, both small and great, rich and poor, free and bond, to receive a mark in their right hand, or in their foreheads: And that no man might buy or sell, save he that had the mark, or the name of the beast, or the number of his name. Here is wisdom. Let him that hath understanding count the number of the beast: for it is the number of a man; and his number is six hundred threescore and six. (Revelation 13:16–18)

This particular system will, even secular observers point out, give evil, would-be rulers the control they've long dreamed to have:

> Economist and author William Michael Cunningham, adjunct professor at Georgetown University, points out what money is:
> "The main economic attributes of a technically effective currency rests on three functions:
> 1. as a unit of account,
> 2. a store of value
> 3. and as a medium of exchange."
> A unit of account is a common measure for the value for goods and services, the store of value is the way in which we store wealth in order to transfer purchasing power.
> The "transfer of purchasing power" is exchanging the dollar from my hand to yours—one private transaction with another.
> That is basic economics for us non-economists.
> Why does America need "social control?"
> Pay close attention.
> Last year Joe Biden signed an executive order for digital money or the death knell for cash. It's not surprising.

We know that Biden wants total control over Americans and their money.

For instance, back in October 2021, Biden asked Congress to authorize new bank surveillance measures of Americans to the IRS. He now has what he wanted all along. His $600 reporting to the IRS on digital transactions (Paypal, Venmo, Zelle, etc.).

This executive order piggybacks off of Senator Sherrod Brown's (D-OH) new pro-digital dollar draft: Senate Bill 3571—Banking for All Act.

This is a blatant attempt to control every issue of your life, including your money.

But hey, who cares…

The World Economic Forum says, "You'll own nothing, and you'll be happy."[32]

Digital monetary manipulation will give the devil's man, Antichrist, the control over earth's population, or at least a large portion of it.

The alarm is set for midnight. The prophetic end-times clock now seems to be ticking toward that midnight hour in every sense. That alarm, when it sounds, will be the voice of the Lord shouting: "Come up here!" (Revelation 4:2)

Last-Days Deluge

No matter which way we look, we see thunderheads of the approaching end-time storm. Despite rosy predictions by politicians, scientists, religionists, and philosophers that earth's Golden Age lies just over the next hill or just around the next bend, we hear rumblings and see the lightning that signals ominous things to come. While an infinitely magnificent golden future lies just beyond earth's stormy horizon, such a future will not be produced by fallen humankind, but by Jesus Christ upon His return to put down satanic rebellion and establish His Kingdom.

No matter what the people of the World Economic Forum or any of the New World Order builders believe, human beings will never produce Heaven on earth.

A brief examination of the direction the humanistic flood is sweeping this generation documents that we are gushing down a sin-darkened ravine toward apocalypse.

Wars and Rumors of Wars

War has been a continuing plague within human interaction since the day Cain slew Abel. Rumors of wars are always with us, because, as James wrote:

> From whence come wars and fightings among you? Come they not
> hence, even of your lusts that war in your members? (James 4:1)

The world's concept of peace is never true peace, but merely a lull between episodes of warfare. When so-called peace is enforced, threats of wars and murmurings of hostilities bubble just below the surface of civility. Jesus, in His Olivet Discourse on final prophecies, however, was talking about warfare that will come with greater frequency and ferocity the closer the end of this earth age comes. Wars, followed by rumors of wars, will come much like contractions increase for a woman who is about to give birth.

We don't have to go back very far in the historical record to document that we live in an age of such convulsive activity. Wars on a global scale are the ultimate manifestations of humankind's fallen nature; we simply cannot find peace apart from Christ's atonement. Our natural state harbors violence capable of producing great destruction. One-on-one violence, families warring against each other, gang warfare in our cities, ethnic groups against other ethnic groups—all these confirm that we are witnessing fulfillment of one of Jesus' key final prophecies.

The frightening fact that we now possess, through nuclear weaponry, the capability of destroying all life on earth is proof God's prophetic Word is truth (see Mark 13:20). We're currently witnessing the floodgate of Daniel's prophecy being opened as the book the prophet was long ago told to "shut up" until "the end" is seemingly now wide open.

This generation watches while peace talks between Israel and its hate-filled enemies are in the news regularly. At the center of those talks is pressure by the nations making up the New World Order efforts demanding that Israel give up God's land for a promised peace.

But that demand, when met, will bring destruction, according to Joel 3:2. The Lord will not abide this taking place without great, catastrophic response. He will bring all nations of the world to the killing field of Armageddon.

All this means Jesus Christ is, perhaps very soon, going to step out upon the clouds of glory and shout with the voice of the archangel and the trump of God, calling all believers to Himself.

Has God Given Up?

I have to be honest. When I survey the landscape of human rebellion, I've said inwardly, "It's just not worth trying to save it."

By that, I'm not thinking of the billions of lost souls, but of this system increasingly driven by evil intention, obviously in the grip of the principalities and powers of Ephesians 6:12. In speaking with others interested in Bible prophecy (and it is an increasing number, I've found) I encounter the same attitude at times: "Why not just give up and let them have the planet? That is, let 'em have what's coming to 'em…"

One recent issue that feeds this wrongful attitude is the frustration engendered by apostate defectors of those who are supposed to be at the top of Christendom.

At the same time, the very word "Christendom" is, in my opinion, a word created by the humanist vernacular corrupters who include every strange wind of doctrine within this terminology. In fact, the term postures the apostates for their imposition upon the end-times religious landscape. The following, I hope, will demonstrate the point.

ROME—We humans "must repent and modify our lifestyles" because of our abuse of Mother Earth, Pope Francis states in a message released Thursday.

In his Message for the Celebration of the World Day of Prayer for the Care of Creation, the pontiff decries the "mistreatment" of our common home stemming from "our consumerist excesses," "tyrannical anthropocentrism," "predatory economic interests," and "short sighted and selfish actions" leading to "the collapse of our planet's ecosystems."

"In the first place, it is our sister, mother earth, who cries out. Prey to our consumerist excesses, she weeps and implores us to put an end to our abuses and to her destruction," Francis declares in his Message.

Because of human irresponsibility "countless species are dying out and their hymns of praise silenced," the pope laments, while the ancestral lands of indigenous peoples "are being invaded and devastated on all sides, provoking a cry that rises up to heaven.'"

Because of the "climate crisis," the poor disproportionately suffer the impact of "the drought, flooding, hurricanes and heat waves that are becoming ever more intense and frequent," the Pope asserts.[33]

The article contained much more—all pointing to Mother Earth worship and agreement with the globalist mantra of climate change as the number-one crisis facing humankind. It is the same madness spewed incessantly by those who sit in the high places of Ephesians 6: 12. And these are the same human minions who occupy the seats of power within the WEF and the political powers that be within the United States who tell us we must suffer along with the world in order to keep from murdering the planet—the same ideological types of wickedness and evil that institutionalize the murder of millions of babies in the wombs of their mothers each year.

> Because that, when they knew God, they glorified him not as God, neither were thankful; but became vain in their imaginations, and their foolish heart was darkened. Professing themselves to be wise, they became fools, and changed the glory of the uncorruptible God into an image made like to corruptible man, and to birds, and fourfooted beasts, and creeping things. Wherefore God also gave them up to uncleanness through the lusts of their own hearts, to dishonour their own bodies between themselves: Who changed the truth of God into a lie, and worshipped and served the creature more than the Creator, who is blessed for ever. Amen. (Romans 1:21–25)

So, it is with this type of thinking, foisted by the likes of this apostate pope, that makes me sometimes say, "Why not just let 'em have it? Scripture says when they worship the creation more than the Creator, God gives up on them, doesn't it? Why not just concentrate on putting out the Gospel message and not worry about trying to correct the satanic evil storming upon this doomed planet?"

Then the conviction comes from the Holy Spirit: "God is God and you are not. He hasn't given up, and He will not until the prophecies are fulfilled. Who are you to do so? You are to be salt and light. Salt is a preservative, and you are here to delay the complete corruption that is coming—*delay*, not stop, the decay. You are to be light in an ever-darkening world of rebellion against the Creator of all things."

Points well made and understood. And points taken to heart.

God does not change, and His Word tells us that today like He did the prophets of Israel as given in Ezekiel 3:17–19. This, of course, isn't to say we are prophets in that Old or New Testament sense, but we are to watch (Mark 13:37) for Christ's return. We do so by observing the times and seasons, unlike the Judaizers who weren't paying attention, thus missed their Messiah's coming in the First Advent.

We are responsible for getting out the prophetic Word of warning in these closing days of the age. We are not to give up or give in, because the Lord we serve says otherwise. We are charged by that same Lord to *forthtell*—that is, to put forth the message of His wonderful offer of grace so you, too, if you don't know Jesus as Savior, can be urged by the Holy Spirit to accept Him this very moment. You will then have the promise of going to Heaven and to be gloriously alive forever with all of God's riches as your inheritance.

14

Armageddon's Alarm Clock

JOHN THE APOSTLE'S WORDS are ringing louder and more succinctly than ever in the senses of those alert to the deceptive siren song of replacement theology:

> Little children, it is the last time: and as ye have heard that anti-christ shall come, even now are there many antichrists; whereby we know that it is the last time. They went out from us, but they were not of us; for if they had been of us, they would no doubt have continued with us: but they went out, that they might be made manifest that they were not all of us. (1 John 2:18–19)

It was already the "last time" when John wrote this under inspiration of the Holy Spirit. The apostle who was so close to Jesus told us just how near Christ's return is. Even though it has been almost two millennia, in God's economy of time, that is nothing. Proof of it being the last time was the fact that there were "many antichrists" in and around Jerusalem. The coming of *the* Antichrist—the final, ultimate Antichrist—was on the way. But, John went on to say:

> And every spirit that confesseth not that Jesus Christ is come in the flesh is not of God: and this is that spirit of antichrist, whereof

ye have heard that it should come; and even now already is it in the world. (1 John 4:3)

Following the Crucifixion, many were at first claiming they believed Jesus had been the Jews' Messiah. They seemed to be genuine followers of Jesus. But, the farther away the time of Christ's death, burial, and well-known Resurrection got, the more these people drifted away from the truth that indeed Jesus of Nazareth had come into Jewish flesh—the God/Man—to die on the cross as a once-and-for-all sacrifice for sin.

Now, those claiming to be believers were feeling the pressures and heat of the atmospherics surrounding the Resurrection. The Romans would tolerate no god but Caesar. The Jewish high-minded religionists persecuted and pursued all who accepted, followed, and worshiped the "imposter Jew" who had claimed to be Israel's Messiah. The Judaizer Saul, of course, was one who persecuted true believers, but he would soon become Christ's most fervent evangelist.

John said those who denied that Jesus had come in the flesh to seek and save the lost were "antichrists." They had the "antichrist" spirit. This "spirit of antichrist" is more and more in view today. For example, there is a massive denial that Israel, the Jews in the modern nation and around the world, are any part of God's plans for the restoration of all things. As a matter of fact, many attribute the term "Jew" and God's promises to that people to themselves.

They go so far, in some cases, as to assign the designation "Israel" to the nations of, for example, Great Britain and the United States. They are, they say, part of the ten lost tribes of Israel. In other words, they claim they and/or these nations are the true Jews and the people who claim to be Jews are—well, like those with the antichrist spirit in John's day claimed Jesus to be—imposters.

These are doing the same thing the Judaizers—the hierarchy of the Jewish religionists—were doing in John's day. They are denying any linkage between the Jews and God coming to earth in the form of Jesus the Christ. This is a denial that Christ has come in the flesh—Jewish flesh.

This is a lie from the father of lies that adds to all other lies that constitute the spirit of antichrist.

This spirit is the one that caused the progeny of Abraham, Isaac, and Jacob to be pursued, hated, and murdered throughout the centuries. This is the spirit Satan has used to rage against the chosen people since the promise of the seed that would be raised to destroy him (Genesis 3:15).

It is the spirit of antichrist that boils within Islam today. It is the spirit of antichrist that brought Hitler's Holocaust to the flesh-and-blood Jews—a thing that, unbelievably, is being denied as ever having happened by a number of people who claim to be Christians.

And this is the reason for my rant. The following excerpt is from one of many communications I get from around the world—mostly from folks claiming to be Christians, and, I might add, those claiming to be the true Jews today—replacing the Jews who can claim genetic ties to Jacob, who became Israel.

The diatribe was much longer than I can devote to this limited space. But, this is the gist, and typical of what I get incessantly from those who say we who believe in the Rapture and support the rights of a phony Israel to exist are, well, headed for a devil's Hell. The person sending this follows a "ministry" that holds to the British Israel theory, or to a theory that the Church has replaced the Jews—modern Israel—in God's promises. He tells about a man who gives the following "testimony":

I have done my own research, and I have been to the concentration camp Dachau four times; once in college, and three times when I was in the military.

I had some problems with what I saw, and with what I was told. I am going to attempt to clarify myself hopefully in an outline that is understandable.

First: 1) I stood in what I was told was the gas chamber; but it was concealed as a large shower room. One question I had was very simple. Why would the Germans use a shower to conceal the gas chamber? If your [sic] going to kill the people with gas; then just do it, don't try to disguise it. There I stood in the middle of this large room looking at the shower heads; and I could smell gas; but was it coming from a vent, an outside source, or what. I couldn't tell. I thought this was somewhat strange. I even went outside the building looking for an outside source, or some kind of piping that would funnel any foreign objects into the building, but I couldn't find any. Actually, the gas smelled like the gas that came from the canisters that we used in combat training when I was in the military.

It wasn't until 12 years later when I was in the Air National Guard; and I went to Widmund Germany to support a Tactical Command fighter unit out of North Carolina, that I really started questioning what I was told earlier. I was in a combat communications unit, and in 1985 I had to go to the Air Force combat communications training school at Tinker AFB Oklahoma....

I went through training in the classroom; being trained in CPR, first aid, Geneva Convention, and so forth, and then I went out into the field for three weeks training in combat.

This was the first time I was ever in the full MOP suite (gas mask, boots, and the entire ensemble) while in training. I was in a foxhole for six hours under the hot Oklahoma sun. One thing I was taught was that in order to have a successful gas attack; there [have] to be nearly perfect weather conditions.

In other words, to[o] much wind could blow the gas that you directed at another country right back at you; and also, the rain has a way of dissolving or nullifying chemical, bacterial, and nuclear gas agents. One thing I learned was that water and steam could very well nullify any gas in the area. I started thinking, than [sic] how could the German's [sic] gas the Jews while they were taking showers? They couldn't, the water and steam would dissolve the gas to the point that the gas would be neutralized.

I realize that it is a terrible thing to come against the Jews; after all, wasn't Jesus Christ a Jew? Wasn't the Jews God's chosen people? And wasn't the Word of God given to the Jews for them to study, and use to bring the light of the Gospel to the world? The answer of course is, NO!!!

This same antichrist spirit is flagrant among those who claim devotion to Christ. In addition to unbelievers denying that God sent His Only Son to die for the sin of humankind, even some Christians who are the flesh-and-blood "chosen people" into which the son of God was born exhibit the *antichrist spirit*. It is this spirit that will bring about the ultimate Beast—the Antichrist. Jeremiah spoke of this in his prophecy about Israel during the Tribulation:

> Alas! for that day is great, so that none is like it: it is even the time
> of Jacob's trouble; but he shall be saved out of it. (Jeremiah 30:7)

The spirit of antichrist is on a rampage, even in subdued ways among the Church, by refusing to address the hatred coming against modern Israel. It does, indeed, tell us where we are on God's prophetic timeline.

Tribulation Temple Clock Ticking…

The believer's pathways toward the future are illuminated through the prophetic Word of God. Many signs are posted along those paths. God's prophets—of whom Jesus, the Son of God, is greatest—describe things to come with unerring clarity.

The Third Temple, the subject of this section, is one such sign. That Jewish house of worship is prophetically scheduled to be constructed atop the most volatile piece of real estate on the planet. That rocky plot of earth is feared by world diplomats to present the greatest threat to Mideast and world peace.

Mount Moriah, known as the Temple Mount, is a focal point for adherents of the world's three most prominent religions: Judaism,

Christianity, and Islam. Only worshipers within Islam are currently allowed to worship upon this promontory at the southern area of Jerusalem. Merely the hint of the other religions' attempts to conduct worship atop Moriah is met with violence from Muslim militants. It seems inconceivable that a Jewish house of worship can ever be built there.

Yet, there is more than a concept—the matter of wanting to build a Jewish Temple on Moriah. In the thinking of some, it is as good as already done. That's because the God of Heaven has declared it will be built. The nation in the midst of which Moriah sits is absolute proof in the thinking of those who believe the Third Temple is as good as already placed there.

Modern Israel is a miracle entity, guided by the very hand of God through more than 1,900 years of dispersion. The Jewish people endured enemies and persecutions of every description while being brought to return and reestablish their nation on the very ground where ancient Israel surrounded the Temple Mount.

This is yet another proof that God's Word is truth. Bible prophecy said Israel would be punished as a nation and removed completely from the land God promised Abraham, Isaac, and Jacob.

Jesus told His disciples while they sat with Him on the Mount of Olives that not one stone of the Temple would be left upon another. This dismantling took place in AD 70, when the Romans, under General Titus and his father, Emperor Vespasian, destroyed the Jewish Temple. The people were scattered throughout the known world and, as prophesied, were brought back into their own land and reestablished as a nation on May 14, 1948.

Jesus also stated that someday there would be a Temple sitting on Moriah and the deceptive man of sin the Jews would accept—rather than Jesus Christ, their True Messiah—would sit in the Temple, declare himself to be God, and demand worship. This would be right in the middle of the last seven years of human history before Christ will return at Armageddon. With all of the other signals that point to that time shaping up for fulfillment, the Temple in which Antichrist will sit must be somewhere upon the end-times horizon.

Those who visit Jerusalem can go to the Temple Institute near Moriah and view all of the implements already prepared for Temple worship to begin. It's more than rumor, I believe, that a Third Temple sits in modular form somewhere nearby and can be quickly assembled once the go-ahead is given.

And, most recently, we see the reason for this subhead title. Certain cleansing rituals must take place for the sacrificial system demanded by Torah. This involves the burnt ashes of a perfect red heifer, which are to be mixed with water for the cleansing practices.

There have been searches over the years for such a "perfect" red heifer. A number of years ago, those responsible for the search thought they had found one. Her name was Melody, as I recall. But hairs other than red were found on her, and the search resumed.

Now they believe they've found five candidates for the red-heifer ritual cleansing requirements. The following, although the Hebrew language can't be understood by most, I realize, gives information about the matter.

The Temple Institute launched its Red Heifer program about a decade ago, led by Rabbi Azariah Ariel. But even in Temple times, an animal that fulfilled the Biblical requirements was exceedingly rare. Failing to produce a suitable candidate from ranchers in Israel, The Temple Institute began investigating alternative sources for a red heifer.

Boneh Israel, an organization that connects Christian lovers of Israel to the Holy Land, stepped in to help. Led by Byron Stinson, a native Texan, Boneh Israel understood ranchers.

"I didn't set out to do this, but right now, I am probably the best red heifer hunter in Texas," Byron quipped. "The Bible says to bring a red cow to purify Israel, and I may not understand it, but I am just doing what the Bible said."

"The prophecies came true, and the Jews are back in Israel," Byron said. "Now they need to build a Temple. But it's like buying a really nice car. If you don't have the key, you aren't going anywhere. The red heifer is the key to making the Temple work like it's supposed to."

The cows [Byron found and acquired] were between 5–8 months old. To be suitable for the red heifer ceremony, the cow must be two years and one day old, so these heifers will be raised in Israel until they reach the proper age.

Chanan pointed out that last year was 5781 in the Hebrew calendar.

"In Hebrew numerology, this is תשפא. That is an acronym for אדומה פרה שנה תהיה (it will be the year of the red heifer). The cows we are looking at now were conceived last year," Kupietzy said. "This year is תשפ ב, 5782, an acronym for בישראל פרה שנה תהיה (It will be a year for the heifer in Israel). In two weeks we will begin תשפג, 5783, the year in which the ceremony of the Red Heifer will be performed. This is an acronym for גאולה פרה שנה תהיה (It will be a year of the Red Heifer of redemption).[34]

Sadly, all this is preparation for what Jesus called the worst time in all of human history. The Armageddon clock is ticking swiftly toward that time of unimaginable horror. But those who know Christ are promised to be kept out of that time (Revelation 3:10).

Messiah Deja Vu

Most of us have had the strange feeling of thinking we've experienced the same moment before. The sensation is brief and almost entertaining. At my age, I've lived long enough to have had a number of these brain slips back in time, or whatever they are.

One dictionary defines the term:

Déjà vu is a French loanword expressing the feeling that one has lived through the present situation before. It is an anomaly of memory whereby, despite the strong sense of recollection, the time, place, and practical context of the "previous" experience are uncertain or believed to be impossible.

A most pointed malapropism (unintentional, often humorous, misuse) of the term was issued by one of Major League Baseball's most famous malapropists, Yogi Berra. (The other is Casey Stengel.)

Berra, Hall of Fame catcher for the New York Yankees, made the hilarious and now-famous quip using the term during the 1961 baseball season. When Roger Maris and Mickey Mantle were batting third and fourth in the Yankee lineup, many times Roger would hit a home run on his way to eclipsing Babe Ruth's record that year. Mickey, batting right behind him, would also hit a home run. They combined that year for a record of such follow-up home runs.

Yogi, observing from the bench as his teammates homered, turned to somebody and said, right after Mickey followed up Roger's home run with one of his own: "It's *déjà vu* all over again."

Well, the way I intend to present the word and its meaning will, I hope, come across somewhat less obliquely than Yogi's observation on that day. As a matter of fact, the things involved are most serious. The Lord Himself seemed righteously angry at the religionists of His day and the way they ignored their duty to observe and report on the times of their watch.

Here is a description of the incident that stirred the Lord to chastise the Jewish teachers. I wrote the following for our book, *Discerners: Analyzing Converging Prophetic Signs for the End of Days.*

Jesus looked directly and deeply into the eyes of the pious religionists and elitist-legalists (the Pharisees and Sadducees). His omniscient, penetrating, piercing, eyes saw into their very souls. These religious zealots and lawyers sought to disprove the claims by His followers that He was sent from God. They wanted Him to immediately perform a private miracle for them, thinking, no doubt, that He would fail, giving them fodder for their attacks against Him.

In answer to their probing demands that He show them a sign to prove His commission from Heaven, Jesus said:

> When it is evening, ye say, It will be fair weather: for the sky is red. And in the morning, it will be foul weather to day: for the sky is red and lowring. O ye hypocrites, ye can discern the face of the sky; but can ye not discern the signs of the times? (Matthew 16: 2–3)

Jesus was chastising these zealots because they deliberately refused to accept that He fulfilled every prophecy that pointed to Him as Israel's Messiah. He later said about these and the Jewish people, who were misled by them, thus rejected Him as Israel's Mashiach:

> I am come in my Father's name, and ye receive me not: if another shall come in his own name, him ye will receive. (John 5: 43)

Jesus was referring to a time in the Israel of the future that would set in motion the most terrible period of all of human history. It will initiate Daniel's Seventieth Week—the last seven years before Christ's return at Armageddon.

We find the prophecy about this one Israel will accept in Daniel 9:26–27. Israel will make a covenant with this "prince that shall come," which this son of perdition will confirm for that week of years.

The Jewish nation is scheduled, according to Jesus, to experience "*déjà vu* all over again." They will again be led astray in their spiritual blindness to Christ's true messiahship. They will instead fall for the False Messiah, who, really, will come on the scene in a dual configuration: the Antichrist and the False Prophet—the two beasts of Revelation chapter 13.

An interesting young man, whom some of Israel's foremost religious leaders look to in an almost worshipful way, has stepped upon the stage of end-times history. His name is Rav Shlomo Yehuda.

The following explains the Orthodox Jewish leaders looking for a Messiah while continuing to turn a blind eye to the real Messiah:

A recent interview on Israeli radio featured prominent rabbis explaining that the Messiah is just about to reveal himself.

Rabbi Yaakov Zisholtz told religious broadcaster Radio 2000 that Rabbi Chaim Kanievsky (who passed away earlier this year) had told him that he (Kanievsky) was already in direct contact with the Messiah.

To understand why religious Jews are taking this seriously, it's important to know that Rabbi Chaim Kanievsky was considered one of the two or three top rabbis of the ultra-Orthodox Jewish community in Israel.

And Rabbi Zisholtz says that Kanievsky and others of the mystical "concealed" rabbis had tasked him with informing the public of the Messiah's imminent arrival.

Rabbi Zisholtz began his explosive three-hour interview with a warning:

...the process of redemption is about to start happening very quickly and at a fast pace. It is important that people remain calm and steady to act properly in the right time. There is a potential Messiah in every generation and there are righteous men who know precisely who it is. This is, of course, true in this generation. Getting the word out now that the Messiah is closer than ever is a matter of life and death. Haven't you heard of Gog and Magog? That is what is going to happen very soon. Right now, the situation is explosive more than you can possibly imagine.[35]

Many among the rabbinical high clergy apparently believe that Rav Shlomo Yehudah is that long-awaited savior of Israel.

The following gives a glimpse of this man of mystery who has suddenly appeared on the scene at the same time so many signs of the Tribulation are converging. There are reports that he performs miracles and heals terminal diseases, among other wonders.

We're outside, waiting for the Yanuka.

It's silent in the deserted courtyard of the little *shul*, for even though coronavirus restrictions have been eased and the streets have again come to life, most people are in bed at this hour. But we're waiting—and then we see him. Soon we're face to face with this bashful young man who's taken the Torah world by storm—self-effacing, unremarkable in appearance, but so remarkable in the impact he's had on the lives of the thousands who flock to him, hanging on his every word....

Rav Shlomo Yehudah was born in Eretz Yisrael in 1988, an only child born after many years. His paternal grandfather, Rav Shlomo, was a scion of the sages of Yemen and learned with the great *mekubalim* of Jerusalem after he arrived in the Holy Land. His maternal grandfather, Rav Yehudah, made aliyah from Aleppo, Syria....

The family returned to Israel shortly before Shlomo Yehudah s bar mitzvah. At the time, there was a memorial event for a relative, and the family was looking for someone to say words of Torah in honor of the deceased. His father asked him to speak before the assembled, and he agreed, out of respect—but even his father had no idea of the depth of Torah that would pour forth from his young *illui*. As Shlomo Yehudah lowered his head and sought the right words, the thin stream quickly grew into a powerful waterfall. People were astonished.

It was as if they were watching a child possessed. The voice was small and innocent, but the words were those of an accomplished *talmid chacham*—a tapestry of Chumash and Navi, Gemara and Aggadah, every source accurately cited....

When Rav Shlomo Yehudah was 18, he began giving regular *shiurim* in different communities around the country, and it didn't matter if you were *litvish*, *yeshivish*, or *chassidish*—people from all sectors began to flock to him. He married at age 20 and settled in Rishon L'Tzion, where he lives today, and where for the last ten years he's been giving a regular *shiur* and trying to avoid publicity. But two years ago, in response to the directive of *gedolei hador* (some of whom come to his *shiurim*), his *shiurim* have gone public, in halls and auditoriums, sometimes drawing over a thousand people at an event. And there are a lot of surprises too. He often asks the crowd to pick a subject they want him to speak about—and he's off and running, pulling together sources from all over, creating a tapestry of light and wisdom for a spellbound audience.

Israel will again make the mistake of failing to discern the time of their Messiah's appearance. The Jewish religionists are once more leading the people astray as they look to one other than the True Messiah— Jesus Christ. The result will be much worse than a two thousand-plus-year diaspora. The rebellious action will bring the time of Jacob's trouble (Jeremiah 30:7).

Gog-Magog Coalition in Focus

It's like looking at a movie. The creative senses of the film's director force our eyes to initially see a blurred vista—maybe a desert scene. At first, the scene just appears to be a barren waste. Then the camera lens turns, and suddenly the view tightens to precisely frame a group of camels and people moving in the far distance.

The scene is no longer blurry. It is in finely tuned focus, letting the movie watcher know this is a caravan of some sort traversing a desert-like wilderness.

This is the way it seems when we consider a particular Bible prophecy that must be relatively near to its time of fulfillment. The recent geopolitical gyrations in Afghanistan and the Middle East in general seem to be orchestrated by a foreknowing director who is bringing into a sharper image the events setting up the Gog-Magog prophecy.

We know, of course, who that Director is—the God who issued the prophecy in the first place:

> Son of man, set thy face against Gog, the land of Magog, the chief prince of Meshech and Tubal, and prophesy against him, and say, Thus saith the Lord God; Behold I am against thee, O Gog, the chief prince of Meshech and Tubal: And I will turn thee back, and put hooks into thy jaws, and I will bring thee forth, and all thine army, horses and horsemen, all of them clothed with all sorts of armour, even a great company with bucklers and shields, all of them handling swords: Persia, Ethiopia, and Libya with them; all of them with shield and helmet: Gomer, and all his bands; the house of Togarmah of the north quarters, and all his bands: and many people with thee. Be thou prepared, and prepare for thyself, thou, and all thy company that are assembled unto thee, and be thou a guard unto them. After many days thou shalt be visited: in the latter years thou shalt come into the land that is brought back from the sword, and is gathered out of many people, against the mountains of Israel, which have been always waste: but it is brought forth out of the nations, and they shall dwell safely all of them. (Ezekiel 38:2–8)

We have for months—maybe even years now—been observing the Gog-Magog assault force coalescing. It has been a process—with Israel, of course, always at the center. The region is incessantly of concern for the New World Order builders who see Israel as being the holdup to peace in the region and the world.

The United Nations—the majority of its nations—has always voted against the tiny Jewish state in most every issue of conflict involving the nation and its surrounding blood-vowed enemies. Israel has long ago, in effect, become the "burdensome stone and cup of trembling" of Zechariah 12.

Until recently, the United States has, for the most part, stood behind Israel, keeping at bay Satan's efforts to bring the wrath of the entire world down upon God's chosen nation. We've seen some breaches in the friendship between America and Israel that have opened wider, then closed to some extent—for example, when President Barack Obama pushed Israel's Prime Minister Benjamin Netanyahu and Israel, too, away from warm, diplomatic relationship. Then President Donald Trump brought the schism back together for the most part. Still, however, the entrenched US State Department *apparatchiks* have continued holding the Jewish state at arm's length to a large extent.

Now, under the Biden regime, it seems the Middle East—Israel, in particular—is being abandoned, telling Israel it is more or less on its own. It is crucial to note that Afghanistan—the geographical area it occupies—was, like Iran, part of ancient Persia. Afghanistan, in my view, is the epitome of this abandonment. I believe it is a part of shaping the prophetic picture for the near future. The entire "debacle," as it's called by Biden detractors, is bringing the Gog-Magog force into high resolution in a big way—an image that now, I believe, can be seen in ever-sharpening focus.

The following excerpt defines clearly the exact nations at the nucleus of that coalition when all is said and done. China is the exception, but that sinister entity's importance can't be missed in consideration of the overall picture.

The Taliban announced on Monday that they have invited Turkey, China, Pakistan, Iran, Russia and Qatar to participate in a ceremony announcing their new government in Afghanistan.

Russia's TASS News reported:

"The Taliban (outlawed in Russia) that seized power in Afghanistan have invited a number of countries, including Russia, to take part in an event dedicated to the announcement of the composition of the new Afghan government, the group's representative, whose name was not revealed, told the Al Jazeera TV channel on Monday.

"'We have sent invitations to Turkey, China, Russia, Iran, Pakistan and Qatar to take part in the [ceremony] of announcing [the composition of the new Afghan] government,' he said."

The TV channel's interlocutor also noted that the necessary procedures for the announcement of the composition of the new cabinet had been completed by now. He added that the Taliban would create "a regime that will be accepted by the global community and the Afghan people."[37]

Not only is the Gog-Magog coalition now sharply defined, but most every other previous fuzzy image of things coming together for being fulfilled now is beginning to, like the blurry desert movie scene, tighten into focus.

Not the least of prophecies becoming clear is the "kings of the east" prophecy.

Armageddon Tidings

Those in the know among former and active military cast wary eyes toward developments in the Oriental world. Every serious interview that comes forward these days brings the direst of thoughts from these experts who genuinely foresee war with China.

The dragon has awakened, and it is thirsty. This dragon is prophesied to be energized by another serpent, also called "the great red dragon," "Satan," and "the devil." This energizing of China in the prophetic future by the ancient foe of God is found primarily in two places in the book of Revelation.

I and many others, of course, have looked at these numerous times over the years. As a matter of fact, we examined these in a previous chapter of this volume. The first of the relevant passages is found in Revelation 9:

And the sixth angel sounded, and I heard a voice from the four horns of the golden altar which is before God, saying to the sixth angel which had the trumpet, Loose the four angels which are bound in the great river Euphrates. And the four angels were loosed, which were prepared for an hour, and a day, and a month, and a year, for to slay the third part of men. And the number of the army of the horsemen were two hundred thousand thousand: and I heard the number of them (Revelation 9:13–16).

John expanded upon the prophecy in chapter 16:

And the sixth angel poured out his vial upon the great river Euphrates; and the water thereof was dried up, that the way of the kings of the east might be prepared. And I saw three unclean spirits like frogs come out of the mouth of the dragon, and out of the mouth of the beast, and out of the mouth of the false prophet. For they are the spirits of devils, working miracles, which go forth unto the kings of the earth and of the whole world, to gather them to the battle of that great day of God Almighty. (Revelation 16:12–14)

The king of the kings of the east, unless something dramatic happens to change the configuration of things east of the Euphrates, has to be China. It could, by itself, have manned a two hundred-million soldier army even as far back as the 1970s. Today, with the other nations of Asia and their massive populations, the two hundred-million figure presents no problem at all so far as potential for fulfillment of the prophecy is concerned. And, certainly, China exerts hegemony over all of the other nations of its Oriental sphere. Many within the secular news media are beginning to recognize the same things those who watch Bible prophecy and current events have been recognizing for some time. China indeed looks like a major influence on factors that might bring nations into a conflict the size and scope of Armageddon.

Each day brings news of China intruding into waters near Taiwan and flying over Taiwan's air space. The ongoing close encounters of United States and Chinese warships in the South China seas bring disaster ever closer. The Chinese are declaring all of that water territory to be theirs, despite that maritime law and territorial statutes clearly demark waters open to all oceanic ship movements. The Chinese government is obviously provoking many of these dangerous confrontations. Any one of the encounters can bring about an accidental incident that could initiate open warfare between the two nuclear giants.

The present American administration, like in so many other areas of its responsibility, seems clueless as to how to rein in the behemoth of Asia.

There is little doubt in my thinking that China will at some point recapture Taiwan (formerly Formosa). This is because all of the world's powers of the Orient east of the Euphrates are called "the kings of the east." China is to be the *king* of the kings of the east. China will bring all of the Orient into its sphere of domination.

Because of its ravenous ambitions to conquer, China needs ever-increasing energy to fuel its voracious military and commercial lusts. The Chinese really don't care about the general populations of their dictatorship. But they are, it is observed by experts on Sino aspirations, intent on making deals with nations with oil resources, through the fiscal alternatives to the American petroleum dollar. Like the globalists of the World Economic Forum and all others behind the New World Order, China's chief concentration these days is on bringing down the

United States' power and authority over economic matters like world oil resources.

When Antichrist comes to power, "tidings out of the east and out of the north shall trouble him; and he shall go forth with great fury to destroy and utterly to sweep away many" (Daniel 11:44). Increasingly, then, it looks like oil will bring all of the nations into the valley of Jezreel for the showdown at Armageddon. It is as if sin, itself, which invaded humankind with Adam and Eve's disobedience in the Garden of Eden, has to come to its full recompense at this future date of human destiny. The Fall caused all of the garden-like earth, particularly the area of Eden, to begin a degeneration of all plant and animal life. The second law of thermodynamics—entropy—dictates that all things continue to deteriorate. All physical matter turns to dust—or, apparently, to oil.

I don't intend to get into controversy about what creates oil, but scientists believe the great deposits are where massive amounts of vegetable and animal matter have been buried, then compressed under pressure of the eons to produce the fossil fuels we now burn in record amounts every year.

Now, the "dragon" of the Orient—China—is thirsty for its share of the black, incendiary liquid. And, its thirst is potentially beyond even that of the industrialized world of the West. It looks like a showdown is coming.

Sin has brought humankind to this point. It started in the region of Mesopotamia and the Euphrates River, where the Occidental world meets the Oriental. Prophecy says that demarcation line will be breached—supernaturally, I believe—with the drying of the Euphrates, so demon-possessed masses of military forces from the Orient can easily troop to the Valley of Jehoshaphat for a final war before Christ's triumphant return.

Keep your eyes and ears tuned to tidings out of the East in these days ahead, while we move toward the glorious coming of Christ for His saints in the air.

And when you see all these things begin to come to pass, then look up and lift up your head, for your redemption draws near. (Luke 21 28)

15

Business as Usual

WE ARE ENDURING a paradox of supreme importance. That is, America's position these days so near the end of the age is at the same time going along business as usual—and it's undergoing the most wicked of all transitions.

We must believe God in Heaven is looking down upon this fallen sphere and this nation like at He did during the time of antediluvian corruption—the period that included the Tower of Babel rebellion and Sodom and Gomorrah's absolute vileness—and is once again about to push the button of judgment. Yet it is, on the surface of things, business as usual.

We are buying, selling, planting, building, marrying, and all the other things this blessed nation has always done. This is all just like Jesus said it would be at the time of His return to call believers to Him in the air.

Lawlessness and Other Proof

My daily emails and conversations usually include a statement similar to: "With everything going on, we must be very near the end."

This usually means this generation of anti-God rebels must be about

173

to get their comeuppance; God must be fed up much like He was with the likes of the inhabitants at the lower end of the Dead Sea during the days of Lot.

It was a time of evil, debauchery, and violence, as we read in Genesis 19. Jesus gave condemning words by saying the time He returns (that is, when He is next revealed to an unsuspecting world) will be just like it was in Lot's day in Sodom and during Noah's day. (Lot's day in Sodom was a microcosm of what the entire world was like during Noah's day.)

In both instances—Noah's day and Lot's day—God found humankind so repulsive in the way they were acting that He had to destroy all but the very few He found to be righteous. The biblical account says the destruction in both cases was complete. That's the case as we look around today.

The antediluvian world is no more. There's not a trace of it, except perhaps in geographical sites, etc. The cities of Sodom and Gomorrah can't be found, either. We do have proof they existed and were destroyed, however, as we will look at a bit later.

First, it's interesting to consider that Noah's day and Lot's day bore similar characteristics. In this case, we'll look basically at only one similarity: Violence was rampant. Jesus said, by inference, that the time He is next revealed will be in a period of extreme violence. This is because, as we read in Genesis 6, violence filled the whole earth during the time just before the Flood that destroyed all but Noah and his family. It must have indeed been a murderous time, one when everyone did what was right in their own eyes, with little or no attention paid to God's prescription for living.

So we are looking at "proof" of the lawlessness—the violence that stems from throwing off God's Law and instead doing what is right in our own sinful eyes. Is there any evidence that this generation is coursing toward violence of such significant levels? Are we in the time Jesus was talking about in the Olivet Discourse (Matthew 24:36–42 and Luke 17:26–30)? Are we at the very end of God's holy patience, as those earlier generations were?

The following may give us a clue:

Our violent, blood-soaked culture has produced a violent, blood-soaked reality in our streets. The final numbers for 2020 have finally been released by the FBI, and they are stunning.

Prior to last year, the largest one-year increase in the murder rate in the United States was 12.7 percent, and that came all the way back in 1968. Needless to say, many of you that are reading this article were not even alive in 1968. Well, we didn't just break the old record last year. We more than doubled it. According to the FBI's annual report on crime, the nationwide murder rate was up about 29 percent in 2020....

The United States in 2020 experienced the biggest rise in murder since the start of national record-keeping in 1960, according to data gathered by the FBI for its annual report on crime.

The Uniform Crime Report will stand as the official word on an unusually grim year, detailing a rise in murder of around 29%. The previous largest one-year change was a 12.7% increase in 1968.[38]

In our book, *Lawless: End-Times War against the Spirit of Antichrist*, a number of other authors and I delineated the exponential increase in every sort of anti-God activity. Just since the book's recent release, we've witnessed an even greater increase in violence. Thus we must conclude that the answer to the consistent comments in the emails and conversations have proof to back up the near consensus. We are living at the very end of the age.

We see proof that God is dealing with absolute evil people refuse to repent from. For example, consider the following:

Archaeologists have unearthed physical proof of what points to the destruction of Tell el-Hammam in the Jordan valley, the region of Sodom and Gomorrah in the Old Testament, and what they found was really wild. They found evidence of an incredible explosion that occurred in the skies above ancient Sodom, an explosion so intense that building down below were destroyed and things were literally vaporized....

From the *Jerusalem Post*: Tell el-Hammam in the Jordan Valley might have inspired the story of the destruction of Sodom and Gomorrah, according to a new study that has spanned 15 years. In the study, published in the journal *Nature* on Monday, archaeologists researched the remains of Tell el-Hammam in an attempt to discover what destroyed the ancient city during the Middle Bronze Age. During the period, there were roughly 50,000 people living in the area of the Jordan Valley in three cities: Tell el-Hammam, Jericho, and Tell Nimrin, with Tell el-Hammam the biggest of the three, implying that until its destruction, it would have been the political center of the area. Radiocarbon dating dates the destruction to within 50 years of 1650 BCE.

Examination of the remains revealed evidence of a destructive event that involved high temperatures, such as pottery pieces that were melted and boiled on the exterior, but normal on the inside. The buildings of Tell el-Hammam were made of mud bricks, some five stories tall. In the upper part of the city, the destructive force demolished the buildings to the height of their foundations in the walls, and little mud-brick remained. Of the palace that was in this part of the city, the first floor walls and the upper stories are missing, and most of the mud-brick was pulverized.[39]

It is more and more evident that we're in a time similar to when the Lord said, "Enough is enough." Judgment is coming. But for those who believe in Jesus Christ for redemption from sin and rebelliousness, the moment of Christ's shout will instantaneously take all believers into His magnificent presence.

Departure, Disappearance, Devastation

It all seems to be a continuing business as usual and ever-increasing perilous times in this nation so blessed since its founding. Reports tell us the grocery store shelves across America, like Old Mother Hubbard's shelves, are growing increasingly bare. Ships are being kept from entering the harbors to be unloaded on the docks.

Semi tractor-trailer trucks are slow in regaining deliverable capability because truck drivers, during the thick of the pandemic, refused the jabs, and everything began shutting down. We're now told containers from ships continue to have unloading delays. Therefore, foods and other wares are slow in moving to the rest of the nation.

Many workers throughout the country, in most every business, are slow to return to work in the formally accepted way. Some have become victims of largesse given to stay home during the pandemic. Those paydays through stimulus madness are causing workplace, thus supply line, reverberations throughout business interactions. All this is creating production and distribution problems that threaten to totally disrupt society. Prices have risen dramatically while economic pressures are producing...well, the experts aren't sure what. Perhaps inflation, stagflation, recession, depression, or even something worse the world hasn't previously experienced.

Gasoline prices continue to head toward all-time highs at the pumps in some parts of the country because the ideologues who see fossil fuels as killing Mother Earth have shut down the previous presidential administration's successful efforts to make the US once again energy independent. Soon, home energy costs will be so high as to possibly endanger some who live within the hottest and coldest climates of America. The rest of us will—if the environmental wackos have their way—just have to swelter during the heat of summers.

Rolling blackouts because of shutting down coal-fired power plants and even nuclear power plants have already begun taking place. Soon, the entire nation will experience what California and others are going through, making daily life ever more unpleasant. This is the forecast of the dystopian bloggers and podcasters who constantly and consistently prophesy the coming time of unprecedented plunges in living conditions on a planet headed for disaster.

These predict the globalists elite are even now in the process of destroying this, the most advanced and powerful nation ever to exist. They have used COVID-19 and the vaccine mandate tyranny to bring chaos. They've used political shenanigans and stolen elections at every level to bring about cultural and societal changes that are hastening the fall of the nation.

The fall must take place, according to many, in order to bring about the one-world, utopian existence the global architects envision. America is the holdup to progress in the ages-long lust to put all the populations of the world under the despotic thumb of a central, authoritarian, select few.

America's greatest enemies, like China and Russia, many fear, are planning invasions of various kinds—and are even already implementing some of the cyberspace and other less kinetic forms of warfare. It is just a matter of time until all of these outer assaults, along with the internal evil undermining America's foundations at every juncture, bring about the collapse of this great republic.

Those of us who study Bible prophecy from the pre-Trib view see almost exactly the same developments as those who have no particular religious viewpoint. The intent can't be missed as the globalist architects employ their unceasing assaults—particularly on the US, but also against all nation-states that insist on maintaining sovereign territory within defined borders.

We see beyond the fears held by those who have no biblical view—or at least not one that's based on sound interpretation. We know God's judgment is coming. As a matter of fact, Jesus spoke of previous times much like those we are experiencing now. He talked about the days of Noah and the days of Lot, as we've mentioned numerous times.

We've seen that, just as the Lord said, times now are much like they were in Noah's day. Violence fills the whole earth. Every thought of humankind seems to be only focused on evil all the time.

Yet, in America, business continues to go along as usual, for the most part. The threats of severe times ahead forewarning food shortages, complete economic meltdown, and all the rest bombard us daily. Even so, we are buying, selling, building, marrying, planting—doing all the *business-as-usual* things Americans have always done.

It must have been exactly like this for Lot and the people of those doomed cities just before God got totally fed up with the most hideous activities going on just beneath the surface of society's day-to-day routines.

Today is like the time of Lot in Sodom. We don't have to have an extraordinary amount of insight to understand the strange unnaturalness involved with the LGBTQ+ or whatever sexual deviancy pervades our culture and society. We are apparently at the very brink of judgment described by Jesus while on the Mount of Olives those two thousand-something years ago.

Those who believe Christ will call the Church to Himself before that judgment falls understand the time could well be at hand for fulfillment.

The account of that departure (the disappearing of all believers from the earth) is given in 2 Thessalonians 2:3, where we see the Lord speaking of the Day of the Lord and of the man of sin stepping onto the pages of end-times history:

> Let no man deceive you by any means: for that day shall not come, except there come a falling away first, and that man of sin be revealed, the son of perdition.

The "falling away" in this text speaks of a *spatial* or physical departure from one place to another. Others still view this *falling away* as falling away from the faith—belief in Christ as prerequisite for salvation. Thorough study shows that the translators of Bible texts going back to the 1500s and beyond interpret this as *spatial* departure rather than as spiritual defection.

I personally believe it could mean both a spatial and a spiritual departure. What follows that departure is the coming on the scene of Antichrist. We see his foreshadow in every direction on the geopolitical, societal, cultural, and religious landscape of our time.

Jesus said, like in Lot's removal from Sodom, the very day all Christians are removed from earth to the heavenly clouds of glory to be with their Savior and Lord, judgment and seven years of devastation will fall.

He said when we see all of this begin to come to pass, we are to look up and lift our heads. Our redemption will be drawing near.

We who know Jesus Christ as Savior and Lord can only echo God's own glorious declaration:

He which testifieth these things saith, Surely I come quickly. Amen. Even so, come, Lord Jesus. (Revelation 22:20)

America: Babylon's Mirror Image

One of the most frightening descriptions of judgment found in Bible prophecy is set within the seventeenth and eighteenth chapters of Revelation. God's wrath is foretold to fall upon history's most blasphemous and wealthiest religious, political, and socioeconomic humanistic system.

Babylon the Great will be destroyed in a single hour. It will take place at some point during the last seven years of the age leading up to Christ's Second Coming.

The most frequently asked questions by those interested in end-times matters are: "Is America in Bible prophecy?" and, "Why isn't America, certainly considered the greatest nation to this point in history in terms of wealth and material achievement, not in Bible prophecy?"

The most common answer given by teachers and others who view prophecy from the premillennial, pre-Tribulation, *futurist* perspective is: "No." America is *not* found in Bible prophecy. That has most frequently been my own answer to that basic question. The United States of America isn't found within the pages of God's prophetic Word.

I can't answer for others who deal with biblical eschatology (the study of end things). I can only say the US isn't mentioned by *name* anywhere in prophecy.

Whether this most materially blessed nation in history, despite the absence of its name, is somewhere in prophecy is another matter. Regarding that, my thinking has trended in more recent times toward "perhaps."

Babylon, the city second only to Jerusalem as far as the number of times it's mentioned in the Bible, is, of course, at the center of most controversy in the question of whether America is implied in Scripture.

Is the US Babylon the Great?

Despite the adamant answers to this query by some of my colleagues and friends on both sides of the America/Babylon matter, I must say they cannot—nor can I—know for certain. Only history playing out can provide the answer. We don't know the future in detail when speculating upon such peripheral issues. That's reserved exclusively for the God of Heaven.

The unfolding of time, however, always draws things into focus so that prophetic details seem clearer. Recently we've seen ever-increasing magnification showing America's possible inclusion within these end-of-days prophecies.

I am not declaring I think America is Babylon the Great. Like this chapter's title implies, however, our nation being in the "business as usual" mode makes it look more and more like a mirror reflection of that prophesied entity.

Babylon the Great

Let's look at the mysterious entity of Babylon the Great. Its total destruction assuredly describes how it will be the apex nation/city/commercial and religious system of human history:

And the kings of the earth, who have committed fornication and lived deliciously with her, shall bewail her, and lament for her, when they shall see the smoke of her burning, standing afar off for the fear of her torment, saying, Alas, alas that great city Babylon, that mighty city! for in one hour is thy judgment come.

The merchants of these things, which were made rich by her, shall stand afar off for the fear of her torment, weeping and wailing, and saying, Alas, alas that great city, that was clothed in fine linen, and purple, and scarlet, and decked with gold, and precious stones, and pearls!

For in one hour so great riches is come to naught. And every shipmaster, and all the company in ships, and sailors, and as many as trade by sea, stood afar off, and cried when they saw the smoke of her burning, saying, What city is like unto this great city!

And they cast dust on their heads, and cried, weeping and wailing, saying, Alas, alas that great city, wherein were made rich all that had ships in the sea by reason of her costliness! For in one hour is she made desolate (Revelation 18:9–10; 15–19).

There have been great religious and commercial centers throughout history. Some, no doubt, were seen by the merchants of the time and others as wielding great seductive and controlling power as described above. Some have been destroyed, usually by military action. Others—such as in the case of Pompeii, destroyed by the eruption of Vesuvius—have been almost instantly decimated by what many consider the judgment of God.

But, these were all in the past—mostly in the ancient past. There has been no comparable total devastation to such a powerful city or nation in modern times. And, the destruction of Babylon the Great is prophetically scheduled to take place within the context of the last seven years leading up to Christ's Second Advent.

If God's Word is true—and it is truth in every respect—there must be a city, nation, and commercial influence of tremendous magnitude during the time John called the Apocalypse, the "Revelation of Jesus Christ."

We must then, if we're trying to understand whether this generation is near the time of Christ's "Revelation," or Second Coming, ask whether a city-state commercial system as described in Revelation 18 exists.

As a matter of fact, it does. It's the only one on the scene as of right now. Far beyond that fact, the one presently on the scene is unlike any that's ever existed before. The United States of America is, in terms of human achievement and attainment of every conceivable development of material convenience, the absolute apex of all nations of all of history! This isn't being boastful of my nation. It's simply a fact even the most ardent America-hater can't truthfully deny. As my fellow Arkansan, the great philosopher Dizzy Dean, said: "It ain't braggin' if you can do it."

America, blessed beyond all nations, materially speaking—and even spiritually speaking, in some sense—has done it. The United States has achieved greatness that is the envy of the world...and the hatred of the world as well, in many cases.

It is deflating, after saying that, to have to point out this once-great nation has become, perhaps, among the most debauched and debased of human history. Lord Acton said it well: "Power corrupts and absolute power corrupts absolutely." America has achieved power like no other nation-state. It has corrupted itself, possibly beyond redemption.

The primary cause of the fall into corruption is that American society and culture—its people, for the most part—have turned their backs on God. The nation has grown rich and insensitive to God's blessings, His great purposes for bringing into existence this most unique experiment in liberty. Like the Lord's indictment of Babylon the Great, it might be said:

> For all nations have drunk of the wine of the wrath of her fornication, and the kings of the earth have committed fornication with her, and the merchants of the earth are waxed rich through the abundance of her delicacies. (Revelation 18:3)

America is the richest nation that has ever been upon this fallen planet. Jesus told us it is easier for a camel to go through the eye of a needle than for a rich person to "see" the Kingdom of Heaven. The spiritual heart—the minds of the rich—is easily turned from thoughts of the True God of Heaven. These have a difficult time even "seeing" or recognizing things of the Kingdom of Heaven. They, therefore, certainly have an almost impossible challenge in finding the only route to salvation—that found in Romans 10:9–10:

> That if thou shalt confess with thy mouth the Lord Jesus, and shalt believe in thine heart that God hath raised him from the dead, thou shalt be saved. For with the heart man believeth unto righteousness; and with the mouth confession is made unto salvation.

Thankfully, Jesus followed up His dire "camel through the eye of a needle" assessment by stating "with God all things are possible" (Matthew 19:26), meaning the rich can attain salvation because of God's love and grace.

When looking at the America/Babylon the Great question, do we see in Scripture any indication that the doomed religious and commercial city-nation system ever had redeeming qualities?

Perhaps—and it is a big "perhaps."

Based upon the fact that Bible prophecy often has dual reference, usually to a local or immediate circumstance and secondly to a distant circumstance, it is appropriate to wonder if the Babylon mentioned in Jeremiah is a future reference to the Revelation 18 Babylon in the following:

> Babylon hath been a golden cup in the Lord's hand, that made all the earth drunken: the nations have drunken of her wine; therefore the nations are mad. Babylon is suddenly fallen and

destroyed: howl for her; take balm for her pain, if so she may be healed. (Jeremiah 51:7–8)

There is a possibility that this indicates the Babylon to be judged had once been used by God in a good way. Babylon has been a "golden cup." Of course, the next statement is that Babylon nonetheless caused the whole world to drink of its evil, thus making all earth-dwellers "mad."

There also seems to be some room here to believe there is still hope for redemption. Jeremiah says:

Howl for her; take balm for her pain, if so she may be healed.

I believe the declaration that this Babylon referenced has been "a golden cup in the Lord's hand" could easily describe America's usefulness in the matters of exporting the Gospel and of serving as midwife in Israel's rebirth in 1948. I'm not prepared to say this is *definitely* describing the United States, but that it would serve as an apt description of the way God has used this nation. In that sense, America is a mirror image of the Babylon mentioned in the Jeremiah declaration. It is easy, then, as one who loves America, to take some comfort from the prophet's optimistic words suggesting possible redemption.

Admittedly, it is nigh on to impossible to see how Babylon the Great might ever have a chance of redemption because of its gross sinfulness, described in excruciating detail by John. But remember that Saul, the mass murderer of the earliest Christians, found redemption by God's grace. As a matter of fact, we can look at our own sinfulness before coming to Christ to understand that the redemptive process is far above our own thoughts and ways. Praise God!

In the same way we might take comfort from the thought of a balm for the healing of America, if it is indeed a mirror image of Babylon the Great, it is equally troubling to consider the corruption-laden imagery that reflects from that mirror.

America the Not So Beautiful

John announces the vision as he sees the crashing down of Babylon the Great:

> And after these things I saw another angel come down from heaven, having great power; and the earth was lightened with his glory. And he cried mightily with a strong voice, saying, Babylon the great is fallen, is fallen, and is become the habitation of devils, and the hold of every foul spirit, and a cage of every unclean and hateful bird. For all nations have drunk of the wine of the wrath of her fornication, and the kings of the earth have committed fornication with her, and the merchants of the earth are waxed rich through the abundance of her delicacies. (Revelation 18:1–3)

Babylon, if it was indeed once a "golden cup" in the hand of the Lord, certainly is here described as having collapsed to rubble. We don't know exactly who this city-nation commercial system was in its glory days that made it Babylon the Great. But the accumulating evidence in regard to Sodom-like, business-as-usual conduct being carried out at the same time unequalled wicked behavior prevails, America can, in my estimation, legitimately be considered for that role.

Heavenly Conclusion

Salem's Lot, a 1979 movie based on a Stephen King novel by the same name, was about a man who lived in a New England town as a nine-year-old. The town was called Jerusalem and was dubbed Salem by the townspeople for whatever reason.

The novel and movie were about a town filled with evil. Vampires had moved into Salem and were beginning to take over through various demonic actions when the man, as an adult, returned to live there.

King's idea likely came from the Bible story of Sodom. The Bible, of course, says in *spiritual* terms, Jerusalem is as Sodom and Egypt.

And their dead bodies shall lie in the street of the great city, which spiritually is called Sodom and Egypt, where also our Lord was crucified. (Revelation 11:8)

While I thought it was a scary movie, my honorary daughter, Jeanie, made fun of me, laughing at the thought that a grown man could be scared by such a nothing film. I'll let you judge for yourself whether it was scary.

One thing is sure: We are living in times like those of Sodom. We are in the middle of Sodom's lot, in that there are those who, like those around Lot, surround the majority of us, even though their numbers are now in the minority.

Lot and his family, of course, lived within perhaps the most debauched society and culture of any community to exist on the earth. Well... probably not the only one so wicked, but certainly among the worst since the pre-Flood society and culture.

We have gone over many developments toward increasing depravity that have taken place over the years—and over the decades. The homosexual agenda has grown and built into a movement that's taken over the American culture while other cultures considered among the most anti-God have rejected this movement. I give you, for example, the following item:

Russian lawmakers are considering a new law targeting "LGBT propaganda." It would provide for fines of up to $160,000 for promoting non-traditional sexual relations. The draft legislation was submitted to Russia's state Duma on Tuesday and is currently being reviewed by the state building and legislation committee.

It proposes to amend an existing administrative law, which restricts information promoting, what are regarded as non-traditional sexual relations among minors. The new law would pronounce parts of the old legislation obsolete and impose administrative responsibility for LGTB messaging in general.[40]

The Russian law will, if adopted, invoke serious punishments for such activity. And, the Russians aren't the only ones who view the homosexual lifestyle as something their societies and cultures don't need. Many of the Arab nations, under Islamic law, even have the death penalty for such activity.

While most Americans, and most within Western nations, would not make homosexual activity punishable by death, it's more than obvious what this lifestyle deserves, according to the Creator God. Just revisit the account of the fate of Sodom and Gomorrah to understand His verdict in the matter.

Today we are seeing an ever-increasing tolerance for things we would have never stood for a decade ago. Yes, LGBTQ+ and the drag queen and transvestite activities were tolerated and more or less ignored. This is what gave rise to an exponential increase in this activity to the point that their lobby is powerful, even though, like I indicated earlier, they are in the minority.

But today we accept things that are just, to my way of thinking, beyond anything any society should embrace. I'm referring to the assaults on the youngest among our children, as indicated by the items represented here.

New York is showering taxpayer funds on a group that sends drag queens into city schools—often without parental knowledge or consent—even as parents in other states protest increasingly aggressive efforts to expose kids to gender-bending performers.

Last month alone, Drag Story Hour NYC—a nonprofit whose outrageously cross-dressed performers interact with kids as young as 3—earned $46,000 from city contracts for appearances at public schools, street festivals, and libraries, city records show.

Since January, the group has organized 49 drag programs in 34 public elementary, middle, and high schools, it boasted on its website, with appearances in all five boroughs.

"I can't believe this. I am shocked," said public school mom and state Assembly candidate Helen Qiu, whose 11-year-old son attends a Manhattan middle school. "I would be furious if he was exposed without my consent. This is not part of the curriculum."

Since 2018, the group—previously known as Drag Queen Story Hour NYC, before changing its name early this year—has received a total of $207,000 in taxpayer cash....

Cross-dressed performers typically read aloud from a list of books that teach acceptance and inclusion, including children s classics like *Where the Wild Things Are* and *The Rainbow Fish* and some that overtly celebrate gender fluidity, like *The Hips on the Drag Queen Go Swish, Swish, Swish*.

But the expansion into city schools has brought new features to the program, its social media posts reveal.

In April, the elaborately coiffed Harmonica Sunbeam wore a slinky gown to meet with kindergarteners at STAR Academy in Manhattan and color pages from *The Dragtivity Book*, which encourages kids to choose their pronouns and invent drag names. Last week, angry Texas parents protested outside a "Drag the Kids to Pride" event—billed as "a family friendly drag show"—at a North Dallas gay bar called Mister Misster, where children tipped drag queens with dollar bills as they shimmied and sashayed.

Compared with the times in which we find ourselves—like in the times of Lot in Sodom—I guess my much-beloved Jeanie is right. *Salem's Lot wasn't scary at all*.

For the world, this is a very scary time indeed; the worst time in human history, according to Jesus, Himself, is almost upon this generation. Jesus said the conditions of society and culture and time of His coming judgment will be just like when Lot was taken out of Sodom to safety, protecting him and his family from the total destruction that was about to fall upon Sodom and Gomorrah.

For those who are truly Christians, the times shouldn't be scary, but full of great expectation. Instead, the times are a sure signal that we are on the very cusp of being called into Christ's presence at any moment. We see the promise in Jesus own words:

> Let not your heart be troubled: ye believe in God, believe also in me. In my Father's house are many mansions: if it were not so, I would have told you. I go to prepare a place for you. And if I go and prepare a place for you, I will come again, and receive you unto myself; that where I am, there ye may be also. (John 14:1–3)

Heaven Awaits in All Its Glory

The moment we close our eyes when we "fall asleep" (God's description of a Christian's death), we are instantly present with the Lord, Paul the apostle and prophet tells us. And we will not all "sleep," as he further informs:

> Behold, I shew you a mystery; We shall not all sleep, but we shall all be changed, in a moment, in the twinkling of an eye, at the last trump: for the trumpet shall sound, and the dead shall be raised incorruptible, and we shall be changed. For this corruptible must put on incorruption, and this mortal must put on immortality. So when this corruptible shall have put on incorruption, and this mortal shall have put on immortality, then shall be brought to pass the saying that is written, Death is swallowed up in victory. O death, where is thy sting? O grave, where is thy victory? (1 Corinthians 15:51–55) which giveth us the victory through our Lord Jesus Christ.

A particular generation of Christians will never experience the *sting* of death, but will go directly into the presence of Jesus when He calls. That's what the Lord said as recorded in John 14:1–3. This is the "mystery" Paul was given to reveal in the 1 Corinthians 15 account.

Heaven's Unfathomable Riches

Not long ago I had to announce my great friend Bob Rogers going to our heavenly home and how he is now enjoying things beyond which we can imagine.

Not long after I shared with readers through tears comforted by joyful knowledge that Bob is alive forever, I had to announce that his dear wife, Vicki, a wonderful Christian wife, mother, grandmother, and friend, joined her husband after a lengthy bout with illness.

However, both were infinitely more than friends in my heart. We are all part of a special family the Lord put together many years ago. It is a spiritual family relationship rather than biological, and that, to me at least, has always meant it was even more meaningful than if we could have been relatives in the earthly, biological sense.

Their daughter, Angie, is my honorary daughter in every sense. She is also my editor (the best in the world of editing) of many, many years. The children of Angie and husband Kurt (also close to my fatherly heart) are my honorary grandchildren, whom I love as if they were my biological family.

Because of her belief in Jesus Christ and being in God's family, Angie's mom is now together again with Angie's beloved dad and is exulting in a magnificent joy beyond comprehension. We can know this because of the following familiar promise from God's Holy Word:

> But as it is written, Eye hath not seen, nor ear heard, neither have entered into the heart of man, the things which God hath prepared for them that love him. (1 Corinthians 2:9)

We have read in the Holy Word that Jesus said in Heaven we are neither married nor given in marriage. Some might find that to be discouraging. I do not. That's because of the above promise. We are promised more wonderful things when we reach the eternal state of joy than we are capable of imagining. This means the relationships—whether they be earthly friendships and family relationships or marriage partnerships—will have a level of intimacy millions of times more wonderful than any relationships we've had while in these earth-bound bodies.

Like in the earlier case of Bob making the trip to his eternal home, Vicki going to be with her Lord immediately brought up the scriptural promise I've always considered profound to a degree almost beyond my ability to express. Here is that promise. In fact, it's more than a promise. It is a fact right at this moment, not just when we reach that heavenly home:

> The Spirit itself beareth witness with our spirit, that we are the children of God: And if children, then heirs; heirs of God, and joint-heirs with Christ; if so be that we suffer with him, that we may be also glorified together. (Romans 8:16–17).

Do you grasp what this is truly saying? All that God has He has given to His Blessed Son, Jesus. God is telling us here through the Apostle Paul that we—already, in this life—possess all of God's riches, in the exact measure as His Son! Now that is something that I can certainly not get this feeble, full-of-much-age, gray matter around!

God is telling us that we are joint heirs with the Creator of all that is! Jesus was given the power and authority from the Father to make all there is!

> For by him were all things created, that are in heaven, and that are in earth, visible and invisible, whether they be thrones, or dominions, or principalities, or powers: all things were created by him, and for him: And he is before all things, and by him all things consist. (Colossians 1:16–17)

The phrase "by him all things consist" has always given me a sense of the awesome power of our Lord. We are told He created the very substance of all matter. He holds together the atoms and even the elements that make up the atom! If He didn't hold the elements of Creation together, all in existence would fly apart instantaneously.

That's how we can begin to somewhat understand why, when Jesus rode the little donkey into Jerusalem to present Himself as Israel's Messiah, He said if the people didn't praise Him at that time, the very stones would cry out. All of nature—the very elements—obeys our Lord and recognizes Him for who He is!

When we are in Heaven with Bob and Vicki, with each other, and with our wonderful Savior and Lord—our Brother Jesus—we won't just be tiny, unrecognized figures in a Heaven full of billions of souls. We will be people in flesh-and-bone bodies, immortal ones, like Jesus. We will know each other individually and intimately, as God, our omniscient Father, knows each of us and every hair on our heads (which all men among us will have again in abundance)!

As Dr. David Jeremiah might say while preaching fervently, "Can I get a praise?"

Believe It...or Not

"Believe It or Not" was a syndicated newspaper series of brief facts about strange things in the world that ran for decades during the twentieth century. As I recall, each explanation of the strange goings-on was accompanied by an artist's rendering more or less encapsulating the weird story being told.

Later, actor Jack Palance snarled out in his usual villainous voice a TV series telling Ripley's *Believe It or Not* stories. The viewers could make up their own minds about the truth of the stories. However, most had enough evidence to back up their veracity.

These were, of course, for entertainment and were mostly about events that had happened in the distant past, so, more often than not, they had no relevance to the well-being of or potential harm to the reader. You could *believe it…or not.* No further action required.

There is one particular profound fact, however, that—as strange as it might be to some—requires a decision involving total commitment to *belief.* To not *believe* invites personal destiny that is the most devastating imaginable.

This is not some imponderable fact or matter of conjecture. This is the truth we must *believe,* or else we'll face a destiny horrific beyond imagination:

> For God sent not his Son into the world to condemn the world; but that the world through him might be saved. He that believeth on him is not condemned: but he that believeth not is condemned already, because he hath not believed in the name of the only begotten Son of God. (John 3:17–18)

The whispers coming in soothing sounds from the creature that tells people not to believe are a million times more sinister than the snarling admonition by Palance in the TV series. Satan says to each human being facing this all-important decision: "Yea…hath God said?"

The same deception brought sin into the world when the serpent whispered those words and Eve, being deceived, convinced Adam to taste the forbidden fruit of the tree of the knowledge of good and evil. God's Word says we're lost because of that original sin. Satan seductively says God didn't *really* say that, but said something else, because humans can determine their own course toward ultimate destiny.

God created us in His own image. At the same time, He gave us the free will to believe…or not. God doesn't force Himself on us. He didn't create robots. He wants men and women, boys and girls, to love Him because we choose to.

However, there are consequences to that decision, individually. Whether we choose to believe—or not—determines where we will spend eternity. To believe Jesus came into the world not to condemn the world, but to provide the way for the world to be saved through Him is the all-important decision we can make. Our choice sets our personal destiny.

To believe Jesus came to seek and save the lost—those in unbelief—and to accept that He is the only remedy for this lost condition is what God requires to cover our sin that condemns us to an eternity apart from His holy presence.

Sin cannot enter Heaven. That's why Jesus said we must be born again. Otherwise, we can't even see the Kingdom of Heaven, much less enter it.

We must *believe* Jesus died for us to save us from our lost condition, we must *believe* God raised Jesus from death to life, and we must *confess* we believe this (Romans 10:9–10).

Like it or not—*believe it or not*—this is the way, the *only way,* to go to Heaven either upon death or at the Rapture of all *believers.*

It is more important than ever for Christians—*believers*—to share this truth with everyone we meet. Conditions proliferating in every direction point to the any-moment removal of believers from the planet. We must look through God's eyes, being one with Him in Spirit, and point to the one Way He accepts for redemption. Jesus addressed His disciple, Thomas:

> Jesus saith unto him, I am the way, the truth, and the life: no man cometh unto the Father, but by me. (John 14: 6)

Not Nearing Midnight, but Gathering for Glory!

For the believer, the dark clouds pervading this time of Sodom-like wickedness that cause things to look like the days of Lot mean something far different. They harbor brilliant, flashing signals that give Heaven's guarantee of going instantaneously into a glorious eternity of never-ending life in God's family.

> For if we believe that Jesus died and rose again, even so them also which sleep in Jesus will God bring with him. For this we say unto you by the word of the Lord, that we which are alive and remain unto the coming of the Lord shall not prevent them which are asleep. For the Lord himself shall descend from heaven with a shout, with the voice of the archangel, and with the trump of God: and the dead in Christ shall rise first: Then we which are alive and remain shall be caught up together with them in the clouds, to meet the Lord in the air: and so shall we ever be with the Lord. Wherefore comfort one another with these words. (1 Thessalonians 4:14–18)

USE THE QR-CODE BELOW TO ACCESS MANY SPECIAL
DEALS AND PROMOTIONS ON BOOKS
AND FILMS FEATURING DISCOVERY,
PROPHECY, AND THE SUPERNATURAL!

Notes

1. Dave Hunt, "The Pre-Trib Rapture: Is It in the Olivet Discourse?" Pre-Trib Study Group, Dallas, Texas, December, 1998.

2. Ibid.

3. Terry James, *Rapture Ready…Or Not? 15 Reasons This Is the Generation That Will Be Left Behind* (Green Forest, AR: New Leaf Press, 2016).

4. "'Christian' Church to Host LGBT Youth Event with Drag Show, 'Sex Ed' Talk from Planned Parenthood," LifeSite, Rapture Ready News, 5/18/22.

5. Dr. David R. Reagan, "A Prophetic Manifesto: The Death of America," http://www.lamblion.us/2013/06/a-prophetic-manifesto-death-of-america.html.

6. Daymond Duck, "Rejoice! The End Is Near!" https://www.raptureready.com/2023/03/11/rejoice-by-daymond-duck/.

7. William Kilpatrick, "The Devastating Impact of the Premise That People Are Essentially Good," *Frontpage Magazine*, 2/4/22.

8. John Stonestreet and Kasey Leander, "Can We Hack Humans? Should We?" *Christian World View*, 7/12/22.

9. Bob Unruh, "Gay Chorus Threatens: 'We're coming for your children'—'You're correct' that agenda will 'corrupt your kids'," WorldNetDaily, 7/8/21.

10. "Doomsday Clock at Record 90 Seconds to Midnight amid Ukraine Crisis," *The Guardian*.

11. "Queer Is In, Christian Is Out—Boom In LGBT Content for Children," Rapture Ready News.

12. Jonathan Brentner, "Worldwide Phenomenon of Sudden Deaths: The Level of Denial and Deception Is Mindboggling," https://harbingersdaily.

com/worldwide-phenomenon-of-sudden-deaths-the-level-of-denial-and-deception-is-mindboggling.

13. Terri Wu, "In War for Control of Humanity, Thoughts and Emotions Are the Battlefield: Dr. Robert Malone," *Epoch Times*, 3/26/22.

14. Terry James and Pete Garcia, New World Order: Worlds in Collision and the Rebirth of Liberty (Crane, MO: Defender Publishing, 2023).

15. Mark Hankins, "God Laughs at His Enemies," Faith.com.

16. "Reprobate mind," https://www.gotquestions.org.

17. Jack Kinsella, "Misunderstanding the 'Great Escape'," https://www.raptureready.com/2021/08/24/misunderstanding-the-great-escape-by-jack-kinsella/.

18. "Netanyahu to Austin: Israel Will Not Allow Iran to Carry Out Goal of Nuclear Genocide," *The Jewish Press,* JewishPress.com, JNS News Service, 4/12/21.

19. Adam Eliyahu Berkowitz, "Iran's Main Nuclear Site Mysteriously Suffers Power Outage Right after Advanced Centrifuges Go Online," *Israel News Mid East*, 4/11/21).

20. Alex Newman, "The Great Reset," thenewamerican.com, 12/29/20.

21. Bill Pan, "Most Americans Don't Trust Teachers, Schools with Children's Gender Identity: Survey," *The Epoch Times*, ZeroHedge, 12/30/21.

22. Adam Eliyahu Berkowitz, "Amazon Reveals Plan to Build 'Tower of Babel' Opposite US Capital," *Biblical News*, 2/10/21.

23. Rapture Ready News, 2/13/23.

24. "Pope Francis: World Government Must Rule U.S. 'For Their Own Good,'" JEWSNEWS, Rapture Ready News, 2/11/18.

25. Timothy Meads, "House Chaplain Casts Out Demons During Morning Prayer in Capitol," Townhall.com, posted on raptureready.com, 7/19/19.

26. Michael Hile, "The United States and God's Judgment."

27. Tierin-Rose Mandelburg, "Biden Calls It "Sinful" to NOT Mutilate Trans Kids," Newsbusters, 3/13/23.

28. Patrick Tucker, "Defense Intel Chief Worried about Chinese 'Integration of Human and Machines'," Defense One, 10/10/18, posted on Rapture Ready News 11/12/21.

29. Daniel Greenfield, "2020 Dems Stand with J Street, Hamas and ISIS Against Israel—Elizabeth Warren, Bernie Sanders Declare War on the Jewish State," *Frontpage*, 11/1/19.

30. Adam Eliyahu Berkowitz, "75% Increase in Anti-Semitic Attacks Spark Fears of New Holocaust in America," Israel365 News, 6/2/21.

31. "The Global Elite's Plan for Your Future: The Great Reset," CBN, 12/8/20.

32. "The Crackdown to End the Dollar Has Begun. Feds Launch Digital Money," One America News, July 2023.

33. "Pope Francis Goes All In! Calls for 'Green Economics,' 'Green Spirituality,' and 'Green Education'! Breitbart News, 5/25/21

34. Adam Eliyahu Berkowitz, "Red Heifers Arrive in Israel," Israel365news, 9/16/22, Rapture Ready News, 9/17/22.

35. Ryan Jones, "Israeli Rabbi Says He's Already Holding Meetings with Messiah," 9/29/22.

36. Aharon Kliger and Aryeh Ehrlich, "Perfect Harmony," *Mishpacha Magazine*, 5/26/20.

37. Jim Hoft, "Taliban Invites Russia, China, Pakistan, Iran, Turkey and Qatar to Ceremony Announcing New Government in Afghanistan," The Gateway Pundit, 9/6/21.

38. Michael Snyder, "The Largest One-Year Increase in Murder in the History of the United States," Prophecy News Watch, 9/24/21.

39. "Archaeologists Discover Physical Proof for Destruction of Sodom and Gomorrah," *Jerusalem Post* and NTEB, 9/23/21.

40. "New Law Targeting 'LGBT propaganda' Introduced in Russia—RT Russia & Former Soviet Union," RT News, 6/10/22.

41. Mary Kay Linge and John Levine, "Over $200K Being Spent on Drag Queen Shows at NYC Schools, Records Show, *New York Post*, 6/8/22.

Printed in the USA
CPSIA information can be obtained
at www.ICGtesting.com
CBHW010708171023
1365CB00001B/1